JUST MY
GAME

JASON GRILLI

FOREWORD BY
CLINT HURDLE

MASCOT® BOOKS

DEDICATION

I am often asked about my ritual of writing in the dirt when I enter a game. "What do you write in the dirt?" A lot of people are with me out there on the mound. Without their strength, support, and spirit, I am alone out there. With them, I am an army of many. I know my family is often sitting up in the stands, and therefore I am never truly alone. There are those who are with me and some who aren't but are in my heart every time I take the ball.

And so as soon as I get to the hill, I write these initials:

TM – Tim Metzger: a family friend whose memory serves as a wake-up call to never take anything for granted. After a heart-wrenching time with the Italian National Team, your sudden passing made me realize that life is too short and that its shortcomings are simply stepping-stones to bigger and better things.

CG – Catherine Giampietro: my grandmother. I have always held a special spot for all my grandparents, but she was unique. Maybe because she always said that the 25 percent Irish part of me set me apart from the other 75 percent. She stood out. She was a rock and supportive of me. No matter how bad something was,

Gram always found the good in me and all my cousins. Doing our best was enough. Those words resonate with me every time I write her initials in the dirt.

JJ – Jayse and Jayden: my two sons. I will live for you. I will die for you. I want the very best for my children. We all do, right? When I put their names in the dirt, it gives me a feeling to fight for the now and the future. Daddy-strength comes when you know the feeling of unconditional love, and I am blessed to know and understand that my job is a sacrifice for them to let me live out my dream. And to my wife, Danielle, the greatest gifts we share are the joys of our two sons. Thank you for your love, devotion, and sacrifice for me. Sharing the joys our sons bring us is the greatest gift you could ever give to me. I want to be the best and for them to be as proud of me as I am of my father, who I vaguely remember watching play, but who is always by my side. I pray that one day you will be proud of your father, and like him, be the men you strive to be.

✝ - I use my faith as my backbone and not my crutch. He is with me at all times, good and bad, and not beckoned when I need Him. Never have I done anything in life without Him.

JMG - Thank you, Mom. Though often living in the shadows, you have played such an important role in my life, my career, and my book. From rarely missing a game to spending your life as the wife and mother of two major leaguers right down to coming up with the name for my book, I can't thank you enough.

I love you all. I also wish to dedicate this book to many, many more. My list is too long to mention here. I hope you know that I appreciate your support.

Copyright ©2014, Jason Grilli

ISBN-10: 1620865424
ISBN-13: 9781620865422
CPSIA Code: PRB0514A

Printed in the United States

www.mascotbooks.com

JUST MY GAME

TABLE OF

CONTENTS

PREFACE

It's not my intention to create a long, egocentric preface to over-dramatize the purpose of this book. I merely want to share my story. You see, I never intended to write a book—well, maybe never is a strong word—but I certainly didn't intend to write one about myself and most definitely not while I was still a participant in the game.

I thought my career was over. Spring training of March 5, 2010, Goodyear, Arizona—I died a death that day. My knee literally ripped to shreds, and I saw my career flash before my eyes in the same way life can flash before your eyes prior to dying. The experience was like a return from death that day, or at the very least from the death of my career.

As part of my own personal therapy, I began writing my journal for my boys, trying to document things I may soon forget as I get further from the unfortunate ending of my career. I viewed this as a way to share stories about my career with my sons, just as my father did with me. When questions about the game or even about life came up during a ride home from one of their Little League games or practices, I'd have my journal to fall back upon. No title, no cover, no graphic design, just lessons about the game and about life that I wanted to share with my sons.

What I reluctantly came to realize, after much encouragement from many others, was that sharing my story could help someone who may need a word of encouragement or inspiration. Perhaps I could teach the very valuable lesson that you are never really done until you quit.

Turning over my personal journal to a friend to read, I was surely apprehensive, yet I was grateful to hear that he couldn't put it down. Watching teammate Evan Meek's eyes get watery as he asked me to share my story one day in the bullpen, I knew I could no longer hide from the media coverage that provoked questions of how a thirty-five to thirty-seven-year-old, former first-round pick stuck it out in the game despite the countless hardships I encountered. I had a snapshot picture of what I wanted my career to look like, but as it turned out, it developed more as a Polaroid picture. It is still developing as we speak.

Everyone has a dream. To reach it, you must go through a journey. This story is just mine. There are many others who reached the same pinnacle and many others who achieved much more than me. This book is therefore aptly titled *Just My Game*.

Thank you to everyone who has supported me and encouraged me to do this the right way. I hope you enjoy reading it as much as I enjoyed living it.

FOREWORD
by Clint Hurdle

It seems only fitting in a baseball sense that I have the privilege and honor of taking the mound as the "starter" for Jason Grilli's book, *Just My Game*. After completing the foreword, I will walk ever so slowly to the mound and place the ball into his capable hands to close out the many chapters that follow. It seems like an appropriate way for Jason's book to commence after the stellar work he has performed for our team over the past seasons. I've had the pleasure of watching him grow, accomplish, and achieve success despite the many unexpected challenges and obstacles he has faced and subsequently overcome. This seems almost natural for me to get the game to where it needs to be so that Jason can come charging onto the field—Pearl Jam blasting—take the ball from me, and put another victory into the "W" column.

I have as much respect for Jason as I do for perhaps anyone in the game. I admire him for his perseverance, his resiliency, and his determination, and I'm honored to participate in his book and in his career as well.

Sometimes in today's world with all of the game analytics, we don't spend enough time on the human analytics. You can't stick a syringe or thermometer in someone and get a true reading. You get a number, but you don't get a real reading. We understand the statistical analysis may increase your chances of winning more than you lose on paper, but we don't pay enough attention to the intangibles, those little things that define the human as a winner. It's those intangibles that more often than not determine the final score of the game more than the runs, the hits, or the errors do. Jason's heart and his intestinal fortitude scream for me. He found a way to continue to dig and persevere, to challenge himself despite facing a disproportionate number of obstacles, and it pushed him to live out a dream, a dream that only he had believed in. He's the classic guy for me to manage, and it is and continues to be my privilege to do so.

When Jason and I were first brought together after his trade from Detroit to Colorado in 2008, I met him out in short right field at Coors Field. I greeted him as I do all new players, and I asked him two simple questions. "What do you want to be in the game? What's your dream?" He looked at me like I had a third eye in the middle of my forehead, as this was obviously not what he expected upon meeting his new skipper. I said, "It's not a trick question, Jason. Tell me what you believe you can do."

And he told me. He looked at me with absolute confidence and said, "To pitch at the end of the game. I know that I can be successful if you give me the chance to pitch at the end of the game." Those intense eyes locked onto mine. "Now don't misunderstand me. If you give me the ball, I'm going to pitch fifth inning, sixth inning, whenever. But you asked me, so I'm going to tell you. I believe if given the chance, I can close games."

Over the years I've asked that question to many ballplayers, and the ones who've told me they want to be great are very few. They've told me many different things, but it isn't every day that someone looks you in the eye and tells you they want to be great. When that happens, it gets your attention. Jason knew that up to that point, he hadn't been great, but he also knew that if given the chance and put in the right position to succeed, he would be just that.

I can remember walking away from that conversation and just saying, "Wow." It was intense, so transparent, and so honest. I hoped that I would be a part of that when it happened and that I would still be around as his manager. I didn't take it as any kind of connect-the-dots situation, but thought that it would really be cool to be around when that happened for him.

Though neither of us were in Colorado when his vision became complete, what is beautiful is if we pay attention, we are prepared for our future through our past by using our eyes and our ears. There are so many lessons and opportunities to learn along the road of life that present themselves and are learned later. I believe there is a natural rhyme and reason for everything that occurs in life. That is why I believe that on Jason's road and on my road, the initial relationship developed in Colorado came full circle a few years later in another environment. It spoke to both of our perseverance, to our passion for the game, and to our commitment to see things through to completion. From that standpoint it seemed to be synchronicity. It seemed to make sense.

One of the reasons the team continued to look for opportunities to give him more was because this whole ride together seemed to make sense to us. We thought maybe there was something bigger involved for him. Within the team concept, I needed to make good decisions not just for him, but for the good of the team. It just worked out that those decisions, all in all, proved to be the same. Jason continued to work hard with the opportunities he had and made the most of each chance he was given. He continued to be successful, so it was easy for us to keep going back to him. The opportunity to give him more was realistic and benefitted both him and the team.

In Colorado, the timing wasn't right for him to immediately step into a more prominent role at the back of the bullpen. We already had guys in place to fill those roles and they were very successful at it. Jason had to continue to work hard, wait his turn, and not lose sight of his dream.

Perhaps part of the road that Jason had to travel was to actually experience the injury in Goodyear. I don't want people to ever think that he didn't have a deep and sincere passion for his profession long before the injury, but there are things in life that challenge us to the core and cut us to the bone. They get us to a place that maybe we couldn't get to by ourselves. His passion was always evident, but coming back from the injury required a motivation and a determination that you could see in his eyes. They screamed, "Just give me the ball and get out of the way. I'm going to get things done for us."

Even after we parted ways, I continued to keep an eye on him from afar and continued to watch his struggles and his battles. I hoped that at some point the opportunity would present itself for us to work together again. When he made his way back to Lehigh Valley in the Phillies organization, some people made me aware of the fact that he was pitching well. He reached out to me a few weeks later and I was all in. Someone else still had to take a look at him to ensure what I was seeing was real and not just a wish on my part. And they did.

What resonates with me is that I knew that Jason knew he could close, but as I expected, he willingly did the work and made his way through the progression to get there. First we gave him the ball in the sixth and he performed there, and then the seventh and he did well there before setting up for relief pitcher Joel Hanrahan throughout the 2012 season. He pitched hard in each role that he was put in and waited patiently until the opportunity presented itself for him to pitch the ninth. When Hanrahan was traded, it was because we had confidence that Jason was prepared to fill that void. I believe it is the first time in baseball history that someone had been given the opportunity to close regularly at that age and, of course, the record shows he made the most of that opportunity.

In addition to his physical skill set, we love watching what Jason has been able to share with the younger pitchers on our staff who look up to and admire him and his story. If I was able to share one thing from Jason's repertoire with younger players, it would be the self-confidence and positive approach to the game that he has maintained throughout his career. Despite countless setbacks, he never stopped believing in himself—and that is very rare in an individual. In an industry that is driven by results, Jason continued to push through despite the fact that he hadn't achieved any real marked success along the way. He continued to find ways to self-motivate, to self-persevere, and with the exception of that one shot at the brass ring on the merry-go-round in Detroit, he never let the pilot light go out. He never let that flame of passion extinguish. He is certainly as mentally tough as any player I've had the privilege of playing with or coaching.

Before and after the game, Jason and I are friends. I've watched him grow up, watched him get married, and watched him have kids. He's witnessed my transition as well. Once the game starts, it is more of a mentality like we are in a foxhole waging war together. If you're in a foxhole with someone, Jason is the guy you want in there with you. He's the guy who will not only cover your back, but will cover your front, too. The trust, respect, and honesty we have for each other is what has turned this into a very special relationship.

Jason's dad, Steve Grilli, was a blue-collar player as well. That was passed on to Jason, which, in turn, resulted in the special love that Jason gives to the game. Steve wasn't all high-fives and trophies. He had to grind and claw for everything he got from the game. The whole family had to move several times during his career and make adjustments. Even today his dad is the guy Jason confides in and asks to help him analyze the game. I think that bond between father and son is what fosters Jason's love for the game as well. After his injury, Steve played a key role in the motivational and inspirational portion of the recovery that proved their father/son relationship was a true gift. The entire family is cut from the same cloth from his mother, to his sister, to his wife, and I suspect right down to Jayse and Jayden. Through and through, they are Grillis.

A prevalent organizational philosophy with the Pirates before I arrived was to include the fathers and the family in what we do. It is my intent and desire to let the players know there is more to life than just playing the game. They're going to be dads. They are sons. They are going to be community leaders a lot longer than they are going to be ballplayers, so it's important that we include the families on occasional road trips and in the many festivities we put together. Midway through 2013, the team invited the fathers to Wrigley Field. This road trip was organizationally significant because it coincided with us having five guys named to the All-Star team, Jason among them. What great timing to have the fathers on the trip with us. They got to be there with their sons and were able to experience the moment their sons were named Major League All-Stars. It was almost as if they themselves had made the team. In many ways, they had. You just can't make that stuff up. It was especially fitting that Steve was there to witness Jason as he was named a first-time All-Star at the age of thirty-six.

Because of his baseball background, Steve's respect for the game dripped all over Jason while he was growing up, and consequently, Jason's passion for the game drips all over the clubhouse and onto his younger teammates. His respect and knowledge of the game is not lost on his teammates, and that makes him a bit of a throwback.

Jason has skins on the wall, and the younger guys see him as that veteran who has earned his wings. He's the old bull. He's seen a lot. He's been through a lot. He's been challenged as dramatically as a player can be challenged in a playing career, both physically and mentally. He's that grizzled old veteran who's been through wars but can still get it done. He's the guy that you don't want to bet against.

The combination of skills and experience at this point in his career makes him the perfect closer for our team. We play hard, we laugh hard, we're all playing to win, nobody is concerned about playing not to lose, and at the end, Grilli is the gunslinger. Shoot or be shot, and the team rallies around him. His actions speak louder than his words. In that clubhouse, we have a very diverse group of men, and all are very respectful of one another's skill sets. They are competitive with one another in a healthy way, and Jason has become one of the team leaders. By no means is he the guy who would lead by calling a meeting, however. In fact, he would back away from being that kind of a clubhouse influence. Instead, he would prefer to simply take the ball and lead by example, simply by getting it done. He's more of a one-on-one guy in the clubhouse and can make an impact without wearing the "C" on his sleeve. He's just one of the guys, but the one who all the guys look up to and look towards for their strength. When you need to get something done, Jason is the guy who is already two steps into doing it, while some guys are just getting up. That's true leadership.

At the end of the game, Jason is the guy we want closing for us. He has a short memory, and that is critical in the make-up of a closer. It's important not to bask in your successes, and certainly paramount not to dwell on your failures. When the game doesn't end as you want it to, it takes a special individual to leave the field, jump in the shower, wash it off, and get ready for the next one. Jason has that ability. He treats every appearance as if the one before it never occurred. His fastball is mid-90s and his breaking ball is swing and miss. If you couple that with his experience, he's exactly the guy you want on the hill with the game on the line. He's got the balls of a burglar out on the mound.

At the same time, he has the intelligence not to get caught up in things when he's successful. He's always the first to admit that it takes runs to win a game. If your team has one more than the other team when they hand you the ball, it's through the efforts of the guys in front of you. Since he has been in the role of the sixth, seventh, and eighth inning guy, he has a great appreciation of what they go through in order to get the closer the ball at the end of the game.

In many ways, when I think of Jason and compare him to other pitchers I've worked with, he reminds me of the late Mark Fidrych. A youthful enthusiasm for the game, a million-dollar smile, and the fact that I can't remember many days where it's been just another day for Jason. Every day, every game is met with a zest for life that makes it seem as if it is his first day experiencing it. I've probably never had another guy quite like him.

So as I hand the ball over to number 39 and allow him to close out the rest of this book, I encourage all readers to strap your seatbelt on tight and enjoy the ride as you experience the game of baseball through the eyes of Jason Grilli.

CHAPTER 1

My Career Was Over Before It Started

> *"We are all faced with problems throughout our lives, some are small, others huge. Depending on how we deal with them, they can be overwhelming and devastate our lives, or they can quickly fade into the past."*
>
> ~ *Anonymous*

The day started no differently than any other during the dog days of spring training. But as the saying goes, it's not where you start that counts, but where you finish. Unfortunately for me, my day and potentially my career ended with me face first in the turf on a conditioning field at the Cleveland Indians' complex in Goodyear, Arizona, writhing in pain and seeing my baseball life flash before my very eyes.

It was a beautiful day, the kind of day that pitchers and catchers dream about. The sky was high, the sun was bright, and a warm, gentle breeze was blowing off the Estrella Mountain Range. I had gotten in my work with the pitchers in my group, and we were ready to wrap up practice at about 11:30 AM on a day I will long remember: March 5, 2010. My golf clubs were in the trunk of my car, and I had every intention of banging out nine on the course as soon as we finished our final running drills. I remember shooting the shit with Jamey Wright, who, along with me, was trying to make the Opening Day roster for his ninth major league team.

A bunch of us lined up on a short field specially designed for running drills, located amidst the batting cages and the minor league fields at the Goodyear Complex. I felt a little tightness in my knee that day during warm-up drills. As a professional athlete, you know your body and gain an inherent trust in it, like a racer trusts his automobile. I trusted my body maybe a bit too much that day and assumed that the tightness was nothing to be concerned about. I took off out of the blocks on a shuttle run as we were finishing up our last few sprints and made it about a third of the way to the finish when my body decided to fail me yet again. I fell face first into the turf, as if I had been hit with a bullet blast, and I felt the most excruciating pain I had ever experienced in my life. I felt as if I had stepped on a landmine as my knee was ripped from the rest of my body. My two previous injuries were to my elbow, and though the surgeries were painful, the injuries themselves were tolerable, considering I have a pretty high threshold for pain. This was like nothing I had ever felt in my life, nor anything I would wish on my worst enemy. I had severed my quad tendon, and my kneecap spun around to face the back of my leg. Every tendon and the ligament structures on the inside of my leg were torn, and my leg looked like something from a Steven Seagal movie when the villain's leg is snapped by a Seagal kick to the tibia. As my knee exploded into pieces, it sounded like plastic crunching when someone steps on an empty water bottle.

My teammates rushed to my aid, and those who weren't too grossed out about what they were witnessing tried to comfort me as I lay face first in the dirt with my hands over my eyes trying to comprehend what had just happened. Like Nancy Kerrigan after she was whacked in the knee with a lead pipe, but hopefully not in the same high-pitched shrill, I began screaming, "Why me? Why does this always happen to me?"

I'd been fighting like heck to get to the backend of the bullpen and to do something significant with my career, and I was finally about to get where I wanted to be. From the time I signed with the Indians, I pushed for a spot on the forty-man roster. They didn't give it to me, because they had to protect some other guys who could have been claimed in the Rule 5 draft. Manager Manny Acta and the Indians' management said they had my spot reserved and said, "Short of Jason stepping on a ball," I was on the team. Though they hadn't sewn my name on the back of my uniform, they had my spot. I was going to help the Indians in some capacity in their bullpen.

I didn't step on a ball, but I may as well have. The explosion where my knee used to be cost me dearly. Instead of making $800K with some built-in incentives to get me just under a million bucks for the year, I was going to be practically standing in the soup line on the Triple A disabled list. Had I been on the forty-man roster, I would have earned my major league salary and earned a year's service time. Instead, I made about sixty grand for the year, or about 1/13 of what I would've made had I been on the major league team. This is just another way the game watches pennies instead of taking care of their investments.

With my face still buried in the Goodyear Stadium grass, memories from my baseball life came rushing toward me. It was like a film projector on fast forward as I contemplated not only the obvious end to my season, but what might likely be the end of my career. After Wright and teammate Tony Sipp got me to my feet and onto the stretcher, the training staff wheeled me to the training room. I lay there, and I couldn't even speak. There I was, out in the middle of Arizona by myself, screaming in pain for my mother, unsure of not only whether I would ever play the game I love again, but whether I would even walk normally again.

The flashbacks continued as I remembered a game in high school where I was playing first base and holding a runner close to the bag. The pitcher threw over a couple times to keep him close, and each time, the runner dove back into the bag to avoid being picked off. On the third attempt, instead of diving back in, the runner jab-stabbed to get back to the bag, and he and I cracked knees. It was a piercing blow. The umpire granted us a time out as each of us "rubbed it off," as instructed by the coach hollering from the bench.

Unbeknownst to me, but held secret for future use against me by my own body, I had chipped a bone in my knee. It had calcified over and remained in my leg for the better part of two decades, then dislodged and shredded my tendon as my body tried to expel it through my skin like a piece of shrapnel. When the orthopedic surgeon pieced me back together, they removed this floating chip—which was the thickness of two thumbnails—from the area formerly known as my knee. I lay there, wondering if my career was over before it ever began.

I lay there on the training table filled with fright and anxiety, surrounded by coaches and teammates who had no idea what to say to me. Pitching coach Tim Belcher, a Big League veteran of thirteen seasons, suggested that I call Danielle because news of my injury was already blasting on Twitter. I wasn't sure what to do, as Danielle was a thousand miles from me and would do nothing but worry once she heard the news.

I was destined to miss an entire season. To make any sort of tangible mark on the game for which I had sacrificed my entire life was now that much more difficult. I had hoped to accomplish so much and to become more than just a one-liner in the baseball encyclopedia. I'd had some shining moments during my career, but to have it ripped away because of a misstep during a training drill was not the way I hoped to leave the game. Every boy envisions himself being carried off the field on his teammates' shoulders in a celebration of revelry, not being carried off on a stretcher, curled up in the fetal position, by the training staff. I was in the conversation to compete for a bullpen position for the Indians with young, live-armed relievers like Chapman and Kimbrel, the budding All-Stars. I didn't just want to attend the dance; I wanted to own the dance floor and be a principal piece in a dominating bullpen.

This was supposed to be the year for me, something I predicted all along. I promised myself and any inhabitants of the world who followed me that the year I turned thirty-three would be my "Prophetic year!" as I continued to wrestle with my relationship with God, like many of us often do. I grew my hair out, even turned my goatee into a beard. Some claimed I looked like I was shooting for the Jesus look (or maybe the look of my friend Johnny Damon from his Red Sox seasons) and in some ways, I was. This year was going to be different than the others. In another ironic twist, I even stepped on a rusty nail while cleaning out my garage during the offseason. This was going to be my season of resurrection. I was feeling great about where I was in life and where my career was finally taking me. I was focused and prepared. I was on this team in Cleveland. It was clear to me that the Indians were excited to have me, and I was pumped to be a part of this organization.

Their bullpen had struggled mightily the previous year, and even the conversations with my coaches and manager Manny Acta during the offseason made me feel they were excited to have someone with my experience. They were counting on me. From a personal standpoint, being close to home was going to be the icing on the cake. Both my family and Danielle's family live in upstate New York.

It was a daytrip to visit, and my wife was going to have help with the day-to-day. My son could finally get to know his loving grandparents and extended family. Though they aren't next-door neighbors, Cleveland to Syracuse was a far cry from the continuous road trip we had been on since Jayse was born in 2008. Since then, we moved from club to club, from Detroit to Colorado to Texas—eight times in a two-year span. Man, you gotta roll with the punches, but it started taking a toll on us as a family. We were so excited to be in Cleveland.

And then it happened—my leg, of all things. Not my elbow or my shoulder, as most might expect from someone who has thrown an infinite number of pitches since age eight. But my leg? Why? What did it mean?

The day was all but over except for conditioning for the pitchers not pitching in the game. We were running "gassers," or suicide runs. I was running straight ahead, and all I did was plant my foot wrong. I guess it was just my time. We can never explain the *why* parts of life. God is in control. I have no reservations about sharing my spirituality throughout, so those who are offended might want to put down the book or perhaps keep on reading because you, too, may need to check in with God. These obstacles are placed in our lives because we all need to learn and grow from them. I surely didn't think I needed another challenge, but who am I to question God? I don't know the answer to why yet, but hopefully it will be revealed soon enough.

"If you want to make God laugh, just tell Him your plans," is a mantra I have used for much of my life, and I was sure this was a God thing! This happened when He thought the time was right, when the Big Man Up Above thought it was appropriate as part of the bigger plan. This apparently happened as part of my journey stemming from something I prayed about a long time ago when I was just a boy.

As I sat in my room surrounded by four walls covered with posters of the guys I idolized, I prayed. I went to bed praying to God for the chance to do this the right way, the old-school way in the steroid era. I asked that I'd be given the chance to do the greatest of things, like my Father, in His name. Life threw me so many curveballs along the way that I often questioned if God was listening or not. They say God doesn't get involved in things like baseball games, but how else can you explain the Red Sox comeback against the Yankees in 2004? I was unsure whether or not I would ever reach my goals, and as I write this it chills me to know that I had to go on such a meandering path to achieve what I prayed for.

My agent Gary Sheffield and I have discussed this very thing in the past. He is so much more than just an agent. He truly cares about me as a player and a human being, not just as a dollar sign. I can't explain what it's like to have Sheff in my corner. We talked for hours, Sheff playing the role of a therapist trying to help me make sense of the whole thing. As I lay on the virtual couch, he helped me realize that in some ways, this injury, coupled with the way I had been misused and utilized in the wrong role, might actually lengthen my career by saving some of the bullets in my arm. Many guys typically fade out at my age because of arm fatigue and the wear and tear of forcing the arm and shoulder to perform the unnatural contortions that throwing a baseball requires. All the innings that should have been logged during my career as a starter and my numerous times on the DL—the disabled list—may have actually worked in my favor. At the age of thirty-six, I was throwing as well as I ever had. The remaining life in my arm had been saved for the famous final scene, my final few seasons on the big stage.

If anything, I could look at this as if I added years to the back end of my career. The wear on my arm was minimal due to the fact that I spent the season away from baseball with a non-arm-related injury. That is truly looking at the glass half full and trying to turn a negative into a positive. My desire to succeed was there, and my skills and velocity had not plummeted. Getting injured is obviously never what you wish for, but if you have to go on the DL at all, it's best to do it while on the major league roster, because at least that counts toward your service time. Not the case for me, as I was simply trying to earn a roster spot. For me, that year was flushed down the shitter: no wins...no losses...no service time.

CHAPTER 2

My Life as an Outlier

"My father gave me the greatest gift anyone could give another person, he believed in me."

~ *Jim Valvano*

Never in my wildest dreams did I envision that I would be nearing the end of my career and thinking back on the ample number of life victories and, though I hate to admit it, the all-too-often defeats that I have experienced during my life. And yet, as I think about it, maybe I don't mind owning up to the defeats. It is those that made me stronger and those that allow me to stand on the mound today as part of the greatest fraternity known to man, that of a professional baseball player.

Like the stats on the back of my baseball card, it seems as if I have scored a few more wins than losses, struck out a few times and made a handful of costly errors. All in all, I'd say my life has a better chance of being considered for the Hall of Fame than my career. In the words of my *paisano*, the incomparable Frank Sinatra, "Regrets,

I've had a few, but then again too few to mention."

Despite what many people may think when they see me pumped with adrenaline after a game-ending punch out, I never have been overly comfortable bringing attention to myself. In fact, when I was in high school, I hated reading the articles about me that appeared on the front page of the local paper the day after Baker High put one in the win column. Dad would run to the front door the second the newsboy tossed the paper and position the *Syracuse Post Standard* carefully on the kitchen table, propped up next to my glass of OJ as he waited impatiently for me to hightail it down the stairs. I'd bound from my room, landing on every other step on the way down, take a couple swigs of juice, wolf down a few forkfuls of scrambled eggs, wipe my face on my sleeve, and head for the door without taking so much as a glance at the headline. All I really wanted to do was get through the school day without embarrassing myself in front of the girl *du jour* I had a crush on at that time. Furthest from my mind was reliving the performance experience I'd lived through just twelve hours before.

I was a skinny kid bordering on gangly with sort of a Ralph Macchio hairstyle. I was quiet, a bit shy, and I didn't really like to be the center of attention, let alone see my name in big, bold type scrawled across the front page of the morning paper. Most guys probably live for that stuff, but not me.

Today I stand about 6'4", weigh in at 225, and fill out my number 39 pretty well. Back in high school, I didn't even consider taking off my shirt in gym class, because no matter how much I tried to gain weight, my food went straight to my toes. There is nothing worse when it comes to impressing the ladies than an underweight Karate-Kid-looking guy with huge feet. When dinnertime rolled around, I would continue to eat long after my family had started clearing the dishes as I tried to scarf down yet another serving. I envisioned that it would help my fastball, my luck with the ladies, and my confidence when I looked in the mirror. My mom was convinced it was so I didn't have to help with the dishes.

Saddled with a lack of self-confidence, I never had many girlfriends through my teenage years. Sure, I liked chasing girls just like everyone else my age, but I wasn't very good at catching them. I was a typical sixteen-year-old, pimple-faced kid overflowing with hormones, but not the typical jock who garnered the kind of attention that many hope for in high school.

When I took the mound, though, things were different. My adrenaline pumped and confidence exploded from the right sleeve of my uniform as I transformed into a beast up on the hill. No longer was I viewed as just an awkward adolescent wearing stirrups and cleats. I knew the moment I stepped on the mound that I had inherited several traits from my old man, and among those were the heart of a winner, a nasty competitive spirit, and a golden right arm.

Where I grew up in the town of Baldwinsville, New York (a suburb of Syracuse), baseball was not the most popular sport. Situated upstate near the Onondaga Indian Reservation, lacrosse was actually the king of sports at my school. I often used to argue with the "lax guys" who would claim their sport was far superior to baseball. "Baseball is for pussies," I would hear tauntingly shouted across the locker room as I got ready for practice. I would shoot right back, "Okay, you enjoy playing professional lacrosse and making $500 a week, while I'm signing my first million-dollar contract." They thought they were right; I knew I was, and ultimately I would have the last laugh. Last time I checked, I don't remember any Baldwinsville boys stealing the headlines while tearing it up in the Major Indoor Lacrosse League.

Dave Winfield, formerly of the Padres, Yankees, Blue Jays, Angels, Twins, Indians, and he-who-accidently-shattered-the-seagull fame, was one of my all-time childhood heroes. He was one of the first to crack the million-dollar salary mark when he signed a ten-year, $23-million contract with the Yankees in 1981. Thirty-two years later, $2.3 million a year is just about what the last guy off the bench earns. How times have changed. When Winfield signed, I distinctly remember a *Sports Illustrated* cover that had the faces of players with their contract amounts underneath. After seeing that, I knew with all my heart that baseball was for me. Not only did I want to grow up and follow in my dad's footsteps, but since I had an inside look into the game from a very young age and knew my earning potential, I was hooked.

Loving baseball as I do, I often sit, scratch my head, and wonder why every kid doesn't love it just as much. Maybe some guys don't like the element of failure, which is such an intrinsic part of the sport. Baseball is very different than any other sport, because although it is a team sport based on the name on the front of your jersey, it is really an individual sport where the name on the back of your jersey is what you are fighting for. Some guys can't deal with the intensity of facing their nemesis in a one-on-one duel where the winner pumps his chest in victory and the loser drags his sorry tail back to the dugout, defeated. Even if that is really a symbolic occurrence, that's how it feels, and some guys can't deal with that psychological pendulum of emotion between success and failure.

Maybe they tried baseball and feared getting hit by a pitch, or perhaps their father rode their asses, making them love to hate the game as they grew up. Too many dads ruin the game for their kids by taking out their own frustration for never making it big on their own. For every "field of dreams" scenario, there is also the opposite: a dad who force-fed his kid, leading to his disdain of the greatest sport ever played. That was not the case for me. Morning, noon, night, eat, breathe, sleep, rain, shine, or Syracuse blizzard, baseball was all I ever thought of.

We lived on a cul-de-sac, and all the older kids in our neighborhood were into hockey. I knew nothing about the sport other than the fact that my friends would get up super early to get ice time, while I despised the cold and opted to stay in bed a bit longer. I didn't mind playing street hockey every once in a while, just to hang out with the guys, but I would ask to be goalie, so that when they shot the tennis ball on the net, I felt like I was at least playing catch with someone. As soon as I saw Dad driving toward the house, I would abandon the pads and we would play catch before coming in for dinner. We ended with a game of "burnout" in which we would throw as hard as we could for as long as we could before exchanging high-fives and taking it in for dinner. It always seemed like a Norman Rockwell moment, as Dad would wrap his arm around my shoulder and we'd walk into the house for dinner. Dad, with his suit jacket hung over his shoulder, and me, carrying both gloves—father and son after a pre-supper catch in the yard. Mom would likely be in the kitchen, dinner getting cold, waiting for her two "boys" to come in from the yard.

We eventually moved from Walpole Lane to Briar Patch, where we lived in the last house on the street in the Radisson Development. The open, untouched land at the end of our street showcased frequent deer sightings and gave me lots of room for exploration, but not much else. I was hopeful to find some kids in the neighborhood to at least have a game of catch with once in a while, but I usually ended up pretending I was Griffey Jr. or Dave Winfield, hitting rocks with an old softball bat for hours on end. Bases loaded, two outs, last of the ninth, and Puckett drives one into the deep, dark Baldwinsville, New York, night. We've all played the game. That became my pastime during the spring of eighth grade when I broke my arm just short of a compound fracture. After sliding into home during a B'Ville freshman game, I assumed that my throwing arm was ruined. Was I ever going to play ball again? It wasn't the last time I ever wondered that, unfortunately—a theme that reared its ugly head multiple times during my career and throughout the pages of my memoirs. I tucked the bat under my chin like a concert violinist, threw up a rock into the air, and hit it skillfully into the night with only my left hand. I spent countless hours hitting rocks into the hot Baldwinsville night. My dad actually still has the bat, and it is dented like the losing jalopy in a demolition derby at the county fair.

I missed a whole summer of Little League that year, and actually got into the hobby of rocketry, of all things. Maybe that tested my will for the first time to continue playing the game. My arm eventually healed, and Dad and I continued playing our intense games of catch out front. As Dad and I both grew older, the bragging rights of his career stats versus mine and who had the better arm became frequent topics of debate. At ages twelve and thirty-five (or so), I have to admit that Dad could still bring it pretty good and likely held Grilli bragging rights.

As years passed, homes started filling out the block, but my body still continued to struggle in the filling-out department. As new houses were constructed, fresh dirt piles helped me come up with a brilliant idea. I set out to build my own mound in the backyard. Here again was a *Karate Kid* moment in my life. After dropping my first load of dirt, I knew this was not a one-day project. Nearly a hundred wheelbarrow loads later, tons of watering and sifting of the dirt for construction nails, I finally completed the task. Placing the rubber on the mound was the crown jewel, for it was now complete. I did not have to ask Dad to play catch on the day it was done. He had been admiring from afar the whole time and was proud that I had completed what I had set out to do. I had geared up for our first bullpen session in the middle of my own "field of dreams." I also built the rock wall that lined the outfield weeds and encased my little slice of heaven. No longer did I just look at the posters on my wall, I now gazed out my window from my upstairs room and looked down at night to see the moon shine upon my newest prized possession. The moonlight reflected off the mound and allowed me to imagine that it was the big, bright stadium lights that I hoped to pitch under one day: Yankee Stadium, Fenway Park, and Dodger Stadium. Maybe that's why I'm not intimidated by those venues today. I pitched in them a thousand times in my imagination before ever making it to the majors. Working on my game no longer consisted of throwing against a wall or garage door; I now had a "field of dreams" in my very own backyard.

During the long, upstate New York winters when the winds howled off Lake Onondaga, I couldn't get outside to play baseball, so my basement served as my holding cell and the bridge between one baseball season's end and the beginning of the next. I wanted nothing more than to be a Major League Baseball player like my dad. Dad's career kind of paralleled mine in that he had to overcome a lot obstacles in order to make it all the way. He was an undrafted free agent, and yet he played eleven years in professional baseball with over two years in the major leagues with the Detroit Tigers and the Toronto Blue Jays.

My father never pushed me to play baseball. He didn't have to. As far back as I can remember, I rummaged through his old Rochester Red Wings duffle bag that sat amidst a bevy of Blue Jays bags that had been gathering dust since the end of his career. Among the locker room that was really our basement, Dad hung on to his old memories and a piece or two of baseball history, including mementos from the longest game in baseball history in which Dad played a significant role. The lure of his old Wilson A2000 gloves that had "Made in USA" stitched to the back of the thumb had a magical mystique that made me fall in love with the sport that I still adore to this day. The cracked leather and nostalgia emanating from one of Dad's gloves made me not only want to be like my dad, but made me realize what I was destined to do with my life. I knew I was supposed to pitch one day and maybe get a glove contract of my very own. It was a rite of passage of sorts. Just as my dad had donned the uniforms worn by Major League Baseball players, I too was destined to button up the front of my shirt, pull the brim of my cap down over my eyes, skip out of the dugout, and toe the rubber to the roar of the hometown crowd.

I often think back to those days and get lost in my life as a twelve-year-old. The moments that I cherish the most are those when Dad and I would head out into the yard to have our catch. Dad spent four years in the Bigs, pitching for the Tigers and the Blue Jays. For much of his career, he wore the number 49, which is the reason I have worn the same for much of my career. I know that seeing the name "Grilli 49" on my back makes Dad think back to his days as a major-league hurler, and it is my tribute to the man whom I respect with every ounce of my being.

Dad's career spanned only four seasons and seventy appearances before he retired at the age of thirty-two. His career record is four wins, three losses, and three saves, and much like my journey, his road to the major leagues was a testament to his desire and perseverance, as he didn't debut until he was twenty-six years old.

Though his career was brief, he still blazed the trail for me to realize that with hard work, a sense of resolve, and determination, it is possible to be counted among the handful of people who have played Major League Baseball. As amazing as this seems, there have been less than 20,000 individuals to play Major League Baseball since its founding in 1871. That's a rather small fraternity, and the realization that two of us are Grillis makes it a rather close-knit group.

One of my fondest childhood memories—and I have many of them—is when the neighborhood kids would ring my doorbell and ask me to come out and trade baseball cards. This was obviously a passion in which many young boys participated. Only a select few, however, are able to pull out a shoebox full of cards with their father's image on the front and trade them for Jose Canseco's or Mark McGwire's. It wouldn't take long for a general manager to lose his job trading Steve Grilli straight up for Canseco, but I used to make that trade at least three or four times a week.

Growing up the son of a Big Leaguer was in many ways no different from just having a good father who worked in any other job. I was exposed to the game and was lucky enough to spend some time in the clubhouses. I don't remember the game itself, so to speak, but I do remember going in the clubhouses after his minor league games and knowing I wanted to be just like Dad. Everyone wants to be just like his or her dad, unless he is a bad father. Fortunately, I was born to a loving dad who just happened to make it to the Big Leagues. It was cool that I got to have a full-time coach, which made me an outlier of baseball.

When I was older, I worked at Dad's bar, Change of Pace, known for the best wings in central New York. As the saying goes, "The Anchor Bar (in Buffalo) invented them, and Change of Pace perfected them." Fans, players, and sports broadcasters don't leave the Syracuse area without a scheduled stop at central New York's number one wing spot. My job, on most days, was cutting the celery, a necessary garnish to go with Syracuse's best wings—along with a large side of bleu cheese. In a Mr.-Miyagi-type moment, Dad set me up in the kitchen on my first day of work to slice four crates of celery. I whipped through them like a 3:00 AM infomercial for the Ginsu knife and assumed my day was complete—until Dad walked me down to the storeroom and showed me carton after carton that still needed to be sliced. Dad quickly made me realize that this was the real world, and there was a big difference between the $100 a week I'd make working in his bar and the money that was out there if I worked hard and pursued my dream of playing professional baseball. The hard work was an investment in not only me, but a payback to my dad and my mom for investing their time, love, and attention into me.

Dad's career was essentially ending when my indoctrination into the sport was just about beginning. Once he left the game, I had a pretty darn good coach. Dad came home from work one day when I was T-ball age, and Mom said she thought it would be nice if Dad would coach his son. At the time, a friend of theirs, Paul Quattrone, was sponsoring a team that played about 150 feet from our house. Then and there, Dad decided to dip his toe into coaching.

After coming home from the first practice, he said to Mom, "I don't think I can do this." Mom inquired why, and Dad replied, "Well, I'm trying to teach them the game and a rabbit showed up in left field, and I lost three-quarters of the team to chase the rabbit." Coming from the level he was used to playing, coaching T-ball was a big adjustment.

Not only was my dad looking out for my best interest and investing a ton of time and energy into my game, but my mom and sister were too. Sports, and especially baseball, were like another religion in our household. We talked about the sport around the clock, and we loved it. Even right down to my mom and sister Stephanie, who worked during the Little League games in the snack shack, with supper often consisting of nothing more than a hot dog, a slice of pizza, and a soda, because we lived at the ball field.

I don't remember Dad being in the Big Leagues, because I was young, probably about two years old, though I do have pictures of me in diapers crawling around the locker-room floor with Dad's Detroit teammate, Mark "The Bird" Fidrych, as well as pictures with Tigers Willie Horton and Ron LeFlore. I do quite vividly remember toward the end of his career in the early 80s when he was winding down with the Syracuse Chiefs. It was like a scene from the movie *Bull Durham*, as I can recall hearing the bus pulling into the Chiefs parking lot after Dad returned from an away game. I remember the roar of the bus and the crunch of gravel on the unpaved streets near the clubhouse. It's a sound that sticks with me to this day and brings me back to everything I love about the game when I hear that sound. My mom would wake Stephanie and me from a sound sleep and drive us to the ballpark late at night in our pajamas after a road trip, because it was like a family reunion of sorts. We would go to pick up dad, and he would bring me into the clubhouse with all the guys who were dumping their bags from the long road trip. Guys didn't have gadgets like iPads and iPods in those days to keep them company on their trips, but many of the guys read comic books. Boomer Wells, who was a teammate of Dad's, would save his comic books for me, and I'd get gum and treats from all the players.

This is one of the goodies in my treasure chest of sights, sounds, and smells that make up my longstanding love affair with baseball. Memories such as my mom having my uniform washed and laid out on my bed before every high school and Little League game, my sister firing short hops in the basement to practice my first baseman position in the winter, driving my parents nuts at night by hitting balls into a blanket I hung from the rafters in our basement, and my days at Seton Hall where I discovered just how good I could be by learning about the history of those who came before me. I remember vividly watching and studying recorded games of Nolan Ryan on VHS. Many an evening was spent attending games at MacArthur Stadium in Syracuse, the home of the Chiefs, and modeling myself after this guy I so admired.

My parents bought a home in Baldwinsville, New York, at the end of my dad's 1978 season with the Toronto Blue Jays AAA affiliate, the Syracuse Chiefs. He ended his career playing for the Rochester Red Wings, the Baltimore Orioles AAA affiliate, in 1981. I appreciate my parents' decision to bring up my sister and me in central New York. Dad was born in Brooklyn, New York, and he and Mom grew up on Long Island. I remember pitching in Shea Stadium and riding the train through Queens and realizing how lucky we were to grow up in rural New York instead of in the heart of the city. That's part of what the journey of baseball does; you never know where you're going to end up. I have never liked the word "journeyman," and truthfully, I don't consider myself to be one. I may have made a lot of pit stops along the way, but I don't consider myself to be a journeyman.

To this day, Dad and I still have our "field of dreams" catch at least once a year. Even at age sixty-three, Dad can still get it up there with some pop. As a kid, I couldn't wait until Dad got home so we could toss it around for a while. I probably didn't give him enough time to unwind from a hard day's work before I tossed him his glove and tried to redden his palm before dinnertime. I couldn't wait to play catch with Dad, especially because I knew he loved it as much as I.

Now, I'm a father to Jayse and Jayden. Jayse has already exhibited an early passion for the game, and I assume his little brother may someday do the same. For now, it's easy to drift into a daydream of playing catch with my guys, who will hopefully talk just as glowingly about their dad as I do about mine. They may or may not grow to love the game as I do. I can only hope. But rest assured, it won't be from lack of time spent with them tossing the ball around in our real-life "field of dreams."

CHAPTER 3

EVERYONE HAS A STORY TO TELL

"If you want a happy ending, that depends, of course, on where you stop your story."

~ *Orson Welles*

People frequently ask me what life is like as a Major League Baseball player. I haven't won a Cy Young Award and never will. I haven't led the league in any statistical category, though I came pretty darn close in 2012 in both holds and Ks per nine innings, and I am near the top of the NL in both saves and Ks per nine in 2013. Fans look at the numbers on the back of my baseball card when selecting their fantasy team. For much of my journey, my stats weren't sexy enough to prove my value as a first-round pick was worth it. I am one of the few guys selected in my draft class who made it to the Big Leagues and spent much of his career without a multi-million-dollar contract. Until now, that is. My career has become a testament to the adage "It's not how you start the race that counts, but how you finish." Though I have never, ever doubted my ability, I have not always been able to showcase that ability.

Many of my fans, friends, and especially my teammates know bits and pieces of my story nearly as well as I do. I often feel a little bit like Forrest Gump as I tell my tales, but rather than sitting at a bus stop with a box of chocolates in my lap, I share my stories with a glove and a bag of sunflower seeds beyond the outfield wall, surrounded by 30,000 screaming fans. Somehow, the mantra, "Life is like a bag of sunflower seeds" never caught on.

I've shared stories of the highlights and lowlights from my career, while my bullpen mates sit in the sunbaked centerfield for hours during each game. This happens because your teammates become your family of sorts, as Pirate late, great Willie Stargell shared when the team adopted Sister Sledge's song, "We are Family," as the team anthem in 1979. I've shared some of the deepest moments of my personal life with them, and they often get to see the real me—not the guy you think you know when you see me on TV or at the park. Not the guy people see striking out more than one of every three batters he faces, pumping his fist wildly as he feels the wind of a "swing and a miss" blow back in his face. That guy is pumped with adrenaline, overflowing with competitive juices and maybe a little too much 5-Hour Energy—not filled with multiple questions about life and insecurities like most of us are. Instead, they get to know the guy who puts his stirrups on the same way as everyone else. They get to know the guy who cries when he is in serious pain and even sometimes when he misses his wife and kids during long road trips. The guy who fought hard to keep together a family that was transplanted throughout the country time and time again, all because of the unpredictable career path he has chosen. The guy who gets angry when he realizes what he worked so hard for was almost stripped away in an instant, just two seasons ago during a freak spring-training injury that left his career and future hanging in jeopardy.

Fulfilling a childhood dream, I was drafted out of high school as a projection pick in the twenty-fourth round by New York in 1994. The Yankees were one of my favorite teams, in addition to the Blue Jays, due in part because Dave Winfield was a Yankee and, as I said earlier, I loved the way he played the game. I had actually been slotted to be picked between the third and fifth rounds by the Cubs, the Rockies, and the Braves, and throughout the course of the draft, each of those teams called my house and asked my dad about my sign-ability. As a high school player, I still had an opportunity to go to college and play ball, making the draft pick more significant to the club that drafted me. No team wants to waste an early-round pick should college be the preference.

As the calls came in from the major league clubs, my dad would ask what money would be in line for the particular round I was being considered. Most of the teams were talking about the third to fifth round. Those rounds commanded as high as $400K to about $200K, respectively, as a signing bonus. After getting a better idea of what pick I was being considered and the figures those rounds warranted, we sat down as a family to discuss my options. My mom who has always kept my perspective on education in focus, made sure the discussion included certain realities. First of all, the fact that I was graduating from high school at seventeen and not mature enough, mentally and physically, should play into my decision. Second, receiving a full ride to college was quite an accomplishment financially. Third, at seventeen, I found out very quickly what taxation on income is and what effect that would have on the actual amount of a signing bonus. Another lesson learned. They say "Father knows best," but in this case, I can honestly say "Mother knows best." As an honor student in high school, Mom wanted us to keep things in perspective. I could attend college for three years and then be eligible for the draft once again. By then, I will have had three years of college education under my belt and grown in maturity, both physically and mentally, to handle a baseball career.

We got a call the second day of the draft informing us that the Yankees had drafted me in the twenty-fourth round. The organization assured me that this pick was no indication of where I should have gone in the draft, but they were willing to negotiate as if I was a fourth or fifth rounder. We were in contact during the next few weeks and based on our discussions, going to college seemed to be the best path to follow.

The day after the June draft was completed, I had baseball practice. My high school coach gathered my team in front of our dugout with a paper bag in his hand. As he addressed the team, he pulled out a Yankee helmet with the NY emblem on it. He wanted to let the team know I had been drafted by the New York Yankees. As excited as I was to have been drafted by the team of my dreams, an uneasy feeling was stirring inside me. The attention was something that always made me feel uncomfortable amongst my peers. I am sure many of my teammates had similar aspirations. Mine was just announced as a reality. I just wanted to go play ball and continue practicing as a team to make our goal of Section Champions our reality.

When the Giants drafted me three years later in the first round, my signing bonus was $1.875 million, so clearly it was a roll of the dice that turned out to work in my favor.

After, Mom sat me down and had me do the Ben Franklin decision-making technique. I opted to stay close to home so that my family could watch me play on occasion while I attended Seton Hall University in South Orange, New Jersey. I felt that if Seton Hall was good enough for players like Mo Vaughn, John Valentin, Craig Biggio, and Matt Morris to attend, then it was good enough for me.

It also didn't hurt that Dad had roomed with and remains good friends with Seton Hall graduate and seventeen-year major league veteran, Rick Cerone. In fact, Cerone was drafted number seven in the first round of the 1975 draft and was the highest Pirates draft pick until I was drafted at number four in 1997.

I had opportunities to go out West or to bigger name schools, including Arizona State, Florida, North Carolina State, and Notre Dame, but there were many reasons that outweighed those when I made the decision to play in a place that was tops in the Northeast for baseball at the time. It was especially important for me to play where my parents and family could come see me play, and because Seton Hall was only a four-hour drive from home, my parents rarely missed a weekend conference game. Seton Hall's mascot was the Pirate, which adds to the irony of my career season in Pittsburgh.

Matt Morris took me under his wing from the moment I entered the Hall, where I majored in baseball and prepared myself for the MLB rather than for a BA, BS, or PhD. I was actually on my recruiting trip as a sixteen-year-old when Morris and some of his Pirates teammates showed me a little of what college life was like. This made me even more secure with my decision to play college ball before turning pro, as college time can serve as that safety net and shields you from a bit of the trouble a kid can get himself into when he is let loose into the world.

My first and only girlfriend was the woman who later would become my wife. She was a senior in high school during my freshman year at college, and though it was challenging, we tried to keep the long-distance relationship going. I missed her and loved her, but ultimately felt that I had to put baseball in the forefront, so we took a brief relationship hiatus. Coach Mike Sheppard called me into his office and sat me down in front of the Wall of Fame that graced the area behind his desk. He pointed out the names Mo

Vaughn, John Valentin, Craig Biggio, and all the guys who played for him and went on to sign as pros, and then he pointed out several guys who had talent but didn't make it.

Shep said, "You know why these guys didn't make it? It's the chippies, women, girls. They were busy chasing chippies. I want you to keep your nose clean, and I don't want to see that happen to you." I think Shep saw something in me and knew the only thing that stood between me and making it was the choices I made. I appreciated him taking the time to pull me aside and look out for me. I think it helped put that little angel on my shoulder anytime I had to make a tough decision in my life. I felt confident that I was going to go in there and play as a freshman instead of having to wait my turn, and I could continue on the path I was steadily bulldozing.

Morris was great to me. He ran with me, pushed me, challenged me, and became almost like a big brother to me. Matt was a junior and was already highly touted to become a pro. This gave me a clearer vision of what it was going to take to get there and where I thought I would go. He became a first-round pick of St. Louis and wound up having a very successful career with the Cardinals and Giants before ending his career as a Pirate. I am beginning to see a pattern here. Having the scouts in the stands to see Morris even benefited me, because though they were there to see him, they saw me pitch, too, and I know I got on their radar despite being only a freshman.

We had a sick team my freshman year, finishing with a record of 38-16. We actually had twelve guys from that team who were drafted, including six of us selected in the 1997 amateur draft. Despite how stacked our team was, we didn't even win the Big East Tournament.

I was selected the Freshman Athlete of the Year for the Big East and named a Freshman All-American, finishing with an 8-2 record with a 1.85 ERA in a very competitive conference. Coming out of high school at 158 pounds and even putting on my freshman fifteen, I only weighed in at 173. I think it proved important to my physical maturity to spend a few years in college before thinking about playing in the pros.

Seton Hall was in a pretty rough area in South Orange, New Jersey, which really opened the eyes of this country kid from Baldwinsville. Going from my safe haven of upstate New York to the ghettos of South Orange was quite an adjustment. Though we were shielded a bit on the college campus, we did leave the grounds every once in a while. If you exited the campus and turned to the right, you may end up face to face with the Newark crowd. If you turned to the left up toward the mall, it was a better area.

Shep would keep us in line, something I didn't appreciate very much then, but certainly understand now. He was an ex-military guy and used to wake us up at the butt-crack of dawn to weed out the guys who weren't taking things seriously. Shep only had to wake you at 6:00 AM a few times before you realized he meant business. He'd have us run one mile and then two and three miles. It didn't take long to figure out who wanted to stay out partying and who wanted to play ball. It sucked for me, because I wasn't really one of the guys who stayed out partying, but still I had to endure the early morning exploits of the Marine Corps drill sergeant. It taught me to be a team player, and even though we all thought that Shep was a little crazy, we also knew he had a method to his madness.

My next year I had a sophomore slump, and I think it was because I tried to do too much. A lot of the team had graduated, and I tried to step up and carry more of the load than I needed to. Unfortunately, it showed in my game, as I became less of a pitcher and tried to be more of a power guy. I finished the season at 5-5 with a 4.25 ERA, which ironically was the same record Morris had in his sophomore year. Though I hoped to follow in his cleats, I could have done so without duplicating his sophomore stink. The team ended at 18-27, which was shameful.

Up until my junior year, I had reached some pretty cool milestones and obtained some accolades while breaking a few records along the way. The best part for me was when I realized that the same scouts that were there for Morris three years earlier were now there for me. During my time there, I held a share of the Big East record for strikeouts in a game with 18, the single-season Seton Hall record with 125 strikeouts, and their career record of 256 strikeouts, despite only playing three seasons before getting drafted. To me, it was never about the personal accomplishments and the record book, however. The only thing that ever mattered to me was the success of the team. I would have gladly given all of that away in exchange for a Big East Championship, and feel the same way today as I chase a World Series ring.

In between my college seasons, I traveled to Massachusetts during the summer months and played in the renowned Cape Cod League. The Cape Cod League is a ten-team, collegiate summer league that has been the part-time residence of thousands of future major leaguers since its founding. I played two seasons there—the summer between my freshman and sophomore year for the Cotuit Kettleers in 1995, and the summer in between my sophomore and junior year for the Brewster Whitecaps in 1996. I remember how amazed I was to be playing in that league, as it is very political and considered one of the premier college summer leagues in the country.

The only downside of the Cape League experience was that I managed to have the host family from hell during my first season there. In leagues like this, the players are put up in local homes in order to keep the team budgets under control. I had a propensity for always managing to end up with, shall we say, challenging host families with mothers who could have auditioned for roles in *Desperate Housewives* and kids who wanted to hang with me as if I were their long-awaited big brother and babysitter. Though that may sound intriguing to some guys, all I wanted to do was play baseball, and I didn't have time to play any of the other roles.

I also had to work part-time each summer and was sentenced to working across the street from the park at a summer baseball camp. I actually hoped that I would get the job cutting grass and landscaping our field, as I could think of nothing better than plopping my ass on a riding mower, eating a sandwich, falling asleep under a tree when my work was done, and working on my tan in between cutting the field a few hours a day. Big Ben Davis, who ended up playing for the Padres, Mariners, and White Sox, had that job, so I was relegated to baseball camp duty. I earned $250 a week, but $160 of it went to the host family for groceries, which was a lot considering their menu consisted of spinach pies and microwave dinners, instead of meat and potatoes or spaghetti and meatballs like I was used to eating at home. For a guy who was 170 pounds and trying to put on some weight to compete against other Division-I players, spinach pies, wheat germ, and alfalfa sprouts were not going to cut it.

Thank God, once again, Matt Morris came around and introduced me to the Carr family, who sort of adopted me and rescued me from the *Nightmare on Elm Street* scenario I was in. The Carrs had some nice toys, like boats and wave runners, but aside from all the gadgets, they were outstanding people. They knew how famished I was and kept my belly full.

The next summer, I was actually supposed to try out for Team Italy and the Italian Olympic Team. I got a crazy phone call from Coach Sheppard right before Christmas break, and he'd received a call from Team Italy saying that I had been extended an offer to play for them. It was an Olympic year, and though I was hopeful that I could try out for Team USA and play for my home country, all I would have to do is prove my Italian lineage, and I would be able to play for the Italians without a tryout. I called my parents and was very excited about playing for the country of my ancestors. We went to New York City to trace our family lineage, and I later got my Italian citizenship and became a dual citizen.

So I was off to Italy for a couple of months to play with the Italian National Team. My town of Baldwinsville gave me a huge sendoff as the local boy who was headed off to the motherland to play in the Olympics. I was on radio, TV news shows, and was treated like a rock star. The dream quickly turned to a nightmare, as the Italian players didn't want us over there and did everything in their power to make our stay miserable. The catchers would tell the batter what pitches were coming so we would fail and get cut from the team. The Italian players petitioned the Italian Olympic Committee and threatened to boycott playing baseball in the Olympics if the American guys were allowed to take spots on the roster from their homegrown players. They had a team full of pitchers who couldn't break a pane of glass, but would rather field a non-competitive team than give up any spots to us.

We knew we were out as marked men, and I honestly could appreciate where they were coming from. We were taking spots from their guys. We were not Italian in their eyes. We were Italian-Americans, or *oriundi*, as they called us in the papers. We made local and national headlines because it became a big issue in Italy.

Dinnertime was especially uncomfortable as we'd sit at this long dinner table with all the Italian players on one end, then a space, and then the three American players, Ryan LaMattina, Todd Incantalupo, and I down at the other end. Though we got to see a lot of Italy, they ultimately sent us home without giving us a chance to play.

We were all at the train station with our big bags packed with two months' worth of gear. There, we joked that we felt like there was a mob hit on us as they shipped us off and threw us away like an empty bag of chips. I was crushed. I cried on the way home, in part because we were treated so poorly, but also because I was slightly embarrassed at returning home to Syracuse just weeks after receiving a ticker tape parade and a five-star send off.

The next year, after I got drafted by the Giants, I was pitching in the Instructional League. During a game against the Mariners, I got to face one of the Italian players who was partially responsible for sending me home. Steam came out of my ears when I saw him step into the batter's box. I can assure you that Claudio Liverziani will never forget that moment. The first chance I got, I did what anyone with Italian blood in his veins would do. I gave him the horns, and I plunked him right between the shoulder blades. I wanted him to drop. As he took first base, I walked over to him and told him, "Welcome to my country now, bitch! *Che cosa fa l'aspetti.*" What goes around comes around.

Later in 2006, when I got the chance to play for Italy once again, Claudio and I met and shook hands. There were many apologies all around, from coaches to players, and the respect was there. Water under the bridge. I finally had my chance to play for Team Italy in the inaugural World Baseball Classic in Orlando, Florida, at Disney. Playing in my own backyard was great.

I started the first game and pitched against Australia in a game we won 10-0. I threw four and one-third innings, giving up one hit and striking out seven. Prior to the game, Tommy Lasorda laid a motivational speech on us about the game and the country we all wore proudly on our chests. It was one of the best speeches I have ever heard, and though I only vaguely remember it, many guys were teary-eyed and emotional. Echoing off the walls of the locker room was the voice of a legend pumping us up on why Italian pride was important. They say when you are around Italians, you become more Italian, even if you are not Italian. In that moment, we all were so proud to be *amicos*. It is the one time in your life when the name on the back of the uniform is what allows you to play for the team on the front of your uniform. For me to finally represent Italy made me believe that all the heartache experienced from ten years prior was well worth the wait.

Three years later, I was lucky enough to be able to play for the motherland once again in the 2009 tournament in Toronto. This was a continuation in the maturation process of not only Team Italia, but also in my own personal growth. We found ourselves in a killer bracket with Venezuela, Canada, and the US. Though we lost to Venezuela in Game 1—where I gave up a home run to my Tigers teammate, Carlos Guillén—we came back to beat Canada in the Skydome, with me picking up a save following three-plus innings of relief against a stacked Canadian lineup that included Justin Morneau, Jason Bay, Joey Votto, Matt Stairs, and Russell Martin. Our squad, which was made up of Nick Punto, Francisco Cervelli, and a bunch of non-major-leaguers, competed with—and got the attention of—the big boys on the big stage. Though we were eliminated by Venezuela in the next game, we took a step toward international baseball relevance.

In 2013, we again took it up a notch after we beat Mexico and Canada to advance to the second round for the first time. I picked up a big save against Mexico in Game 1, which filled me with a great sense of national pride; I proved to myself and the world that I could get it done on the big stage. This catapulted me into the 2013 season, where I would take the ball under many pressure-packed moments as the closer of the Pittsburgh Pirates.

It is amazing how things have changed in the fifteen years that transpired between my premature exit from Italy and how the team has since grown. With my tour of Italy cut short that summer, I returned for a second summer to the Cape Cod League and pitched for the Brewster Whitecaps. I had an off-the-charts summer season, which helped put me on the map as a first-round draft pick the next season. I pitched that summer with a chip on my shoulder, which became a recurring theme throughout my career, and the hitters of the Cape Cod League paid the price. Tell me that I can't, and I'll show you that I can.

As the summer ended, I returned to school and took academics a bit lightly my junior year, as I knew I had to focus on baseball. My course load in the spring semester consisted of twelve credits, including Scuba Diving, Intro to Marketing, Astronomy, and a sculpture class. They were easy-cheesy classes, so I could dedicate my time to my craft before I headed out to chase my career aspirations.

I put it all together my junior year and the team rebounded, finishing at 32-22. I remember every time I'd warm up in the bullpen, I was jacked up because it was my time to shine. Dad used to come to the pen when I was warming up to pump me up, and I pitched games with fifteen, sixteen, and eighteen strikeouts during the season. The day I fanned eighteen was against Connecticut on April 26, 1997. I closed the first game of a doubleheader that day, striking out three guys in an inning and a third. I then came back and started the second game, because we needed to win both games to make the Big East Tournament. I whiffed eighteen in the second game, a day that my curve ball was breaking a foot and a half, and the stands were filled with scouts. If there was ever a time that I needed to shine, that was it. Lucky for me, I came through.

I knew that whenever scouts were known to be in the stands, it was time to show off instead of be nervous. With major league scouts often sitting there with note pads and JUGS Guns, it was my moment to shine and make things happen. Mom and Dad never missed a weekend conference series, as the drive was only four hours from Syracuse, and with the game on the line and my future in front of me, they wouldn't miss a series for the world. Despite the fact that I could have practically owned the campus at that time, I tried to remain humble. Baseball is a game that will teach you humility the moment you start to get overconfident. The phone rang off the hook my junior year with scouts calling and asking me all kinds of questions, and I could tell that my college roommate got sick each time the phone rang and he had to deliver the message to me. He had aspirations of playing pro ball, too, and it became a little uncomfortable when the phone was always ringing for me and never for him. It reminded me of the Black Crowes song "Jealous Again," because it was a repeat performance of what happened to me during my high school years.

I ultimately experienced my dream of being a first-round pick when I was selected at number four by the Giants. It came as a shock only because the Giants never really showed any real interest prior to the draft. I never remembered seeing any scouts around until Alan Marr came to my draft party and became the scout who signed me. I had hoped to be selected early, but never anticipated the Giants being in the mix. They seemed to lurk in the shadows and had made the decision to select me if I was available.

As conceited as it may sound, I would often find an excuse to get in front of a mirror. When I finally put my first Giants jersey on, it made me realize that the hard work actually paid off. There were more carrots to dangle in front of my nose, because the power of positive belief and hard work got me to that point. Now, that same mentality was going to get me where I ultimately wanted to be. I wanted to be in the Big Leagues, not just wear a uniform.

Being picked fourth overall out of 1,607 players who were drafted that year is something I am extremely proud of, along with the realization that I was selected ahead of guys like Vernon Wells, Michael Cuddyer, Jon Garland, Jayson Werth, and Lance Berkman and behind only Matt Anderson, J.D. Drew, and Troy Glaus. None of us are likely to see our faces emblazoned on plaques in Cooperstown, but each of us will forever live with the realization that we are part of the exclusive fraternity of brothers who buttoned up the uniform of a Major League Baseball team. More specifically, we were first-round picks in the class of '97. Being selected in the first-round of the draft is no guarantee that you'll make it to "The Show." On average, only about two out of three first-round picks ever taste a day in the Bigs.

I had some other teams in mind that I hoped would draft me, but I was still ecstatic to be a Giant. The downside was I would be playing ball a long way from home, but this was something that I had no control over, so I made the best of it. I remember when it was announced who drafted me, my mom sat there crying. I know she cried for many reasons, but one was the realization of how far from home I'd really be.

Underneath my bed at home, I had this two-part poster with the Bay Bridge on it. Will Clark of the Giants was on one side and Mark McGwire of the A's on the other side. The poster was from the Bay Bridge World Series in 1989, which was interrupted by the famous earthquake that shut down the city of San Francisco and delayed the continuation of the World Series for ten days. That poster, with Clark, who hit left-handed swinging one way, and McGwire, who was right-handed swinging from the other side, hung over my bed for years. It was serendipitous that for years, I slept under a picture of the bridge that I was hopefully going to see an awful lot of…if my career went as planned.

I am not the type of guy who seeks the spotlight, but there is nothing better than the electricity of the crowd. When I'm on the hill, in the zone, I'm really not affected by the sights and sounds that surround me. Though I can feel the buzz pulsating in the stands. It's like the pull of a magnet; you are unable to see, smell, or hear, but you can feel the energy pushing and pulling you at the same time. For me, there is no better feeling in the world than the one-on-one, *mano-a-mano*, battle of hitter against pitcher. I never have been the type of person who does it for the fame. I think if anything, I hid from that attention as I have always tried to be a little bit private with my life. As I explained earlier, I needed some arm-twisting in order to be convinced to share my story and write this book.

In this lifestyle that I've chosen, maintaining a veil of privacy around oneself is hard to do. With social media, the Internet, ESPN, the MLB Network, and 24/7 news stations, it actually seems damn near impossible. I've actually adopted the motto, "If you can't beat 'em, join 'em," in trying to learn what social media is all about.

I remember my dad giving me a pump-up speech at the chain-link fence after warming up and walking in to start a game. Those moments are forever etched in my brain. He has been my best friend and my biggest fan since day one, and though many may think he lived his career vicariously through me, that couldn't be further from the truth. Dad is proud of his career, and well, he should be.

Dad played about two years in the Bigs, not long enough to be pension-worthy. This is one of the reasons I fight so hard with the MLB Players Association to take care of the old-timers who played the game but haven't been taken care of the way they should have been. To go from a non-drafted free agent to a Big Leaguer and a contract with Snickers is quite an accomplishment. Not only that, but Dad played at Gannon University—a rather small school hardly known as a baseball factory—yet he lives his life knowing that his face is on a baseball card. He just gave it his all, got a shot, and made it to the Big Leagues.

I think that's where I get my love and respect for the game. The tenacity he showed made me realize that, though we may have come from different ends of the spectrum, it was going to take all the heart I could muster to match my Dad's accomplishments and someday see my ugly mug on the front of my own baseball card. Dad taught me to respect the game through his actions as well as his words. During the hip-hop era when every kid was turning their caps backwards like Ken Griffey Jr., Dad would yell at the guys on our team, saying that is not how baseball hats are meant to be worn, especially around the field. The game was to be played right and played hard, and whether that meant hustling out every hit, or raking the field and the mound so it looks better for the next time you play, he made it clear that the game was to be played only one way. Dad treated the sport as if it were sacred, and he taught me to do the same. I've never met anyone who has such a bond with the sport.

It was because of this love for the sport that I decided never to take steroids to recover from injuries or to level the playing field. It was a relatively easy decision. He taught me that guys who cheated the sport by taking steroids would garner the wrong kind of attention, and now they have to pay the consequences for their actions. Their name is defamed, and I can assure you that I will never do anything to defame the name I wear on the back of my jersey. I thought about taking steroids while recovering from my knee injury, but Dad talked me out of succumbing to peer pressure and throwing away everything I always believed in. I'm glad I took Dad's advice, and I was able to sleep better at night knowing I did the right thing. We Grillis may be skinny guys, but we have a lot of guts.

Dad also participated in the longest game in pro baseball history: a thirty-three inning affair between the Rochester Red Wings and the Pawtucket Red Sox. Though Dad wasn't even there for the first thirty-two innings, he said that it was probably the game of his life.

The first thirty-two innings of the game, whose lineup included two future Hall of Famers in Wade Boggs and Cal Ripken, were played on April 18th and into the morning of the 19th, before being called on account of severe fatigue on the part of the players, coaches, umpires, and the handful of fans who remained. The game was continued three months later on the Red Wings' next trip to Pawtucket as the opening end of a double-header. Dad said it was extremely nerve-racking, and there was so much media attention surrounding this minor-league game. Being that he had Big League experience, former Pirates great Doc Ellis, Rochester's manager at the time, told management that he really wanted to win the game. So they put Dad on the roster. He jokes now that what took them over seven hours to do during the first part of the game, he undid in five minutes. By participating in that game, though he ultimately took the loss, he finds himself part of baseball lore, and his Rochester Red Wings hat has a place in Cooperstown at the Baseball Hall of Fame.

He is also a member of the Syracuse Chiefs' Hall of Fame and currently works as the color analyst for the Chiefs' home baseball games. So, despite my career being longer and a bit more glamorous than Dad's, he certainly has never had to live his career through me. He has always been a great coach and has the keen ability to keep me grounded, because he knows the game so well and has seen and lived through much that I haven't yet experienced.

I played basketball in high school, one year of soccer as a kid, and I even did karate for a while. Sports helped to keep me focused and grounded. Mom and Dad said they didn't appreciate my attitude during basketball season. I wanted to win so badly and the game frustrated me to no end. I'd come down to the kitchen table, and Mom and Dad would just look at each other and know that it was basketball season. They found themselves walking on eggshells for the next month or so.

Yet the desire to win is a Grilli trait that I learned from the patriarch himself. To this day, for example, my dad has played table tennis against my young nephew countless times and refuses to let him win, because he believes that a win should be earned, not awarded. As Dad said, "The day he finally beats me, he'll deserve to beat me, and it will be a glorious day." That, in a nutshell, is where the seed was planted that blossomed into my desire to succeed in everything that I do.

Dad managed my junior-varsity team in high school, but when I made it to varsity, they wanted him to continue to coach the JV squad. He didn't want to stay there while I was with the big club, so he was named the varsity pitching coach. When I got drafted by the Yankees, many of those not in the know said it was due to Dad's influence. I was never sure if they were envious or if they believed that was how the system worked, but Big League teams obviously don't give seven figures to players just because their dad played.

I remember the day I walked into the gymnasium at Baker High School in Baldwinsville. Section III Championship banners hung on the wall for every sport except baseball. That became my ultimate goal, and I dreamed of bringing us a Section III Championship banner. I wasn't a rah-rah type of guy, but I wanted more than anything to leave with the patch on my jacket. I didn't have a letter jacket and didn't care to have one, but I was not going to graduate without a championship patch. My senior year, I threw a no-hitter in the Section III Championship game at none other than MacArthur Stadium where my Dad played so many seasons for the Chiefs. The game was against our rival Liverpool, and a brawl occurred after a collision at home plate. The funniest part of that incident was that we were good friends with many of the Liverpool guys. After the high school season ended, the better players would join forces and play summer ball together in tournaments against teams from upstate, like Cicero, Dunkirk, and North Syracuse, and we won a few state championships.

Though not as well known for its baseball as states like Florida, California, and Texas, who are able to play year round, the Central New York region produces players with some pretty solid athletic abilities, and the competition proved to be strong enough to get me ready for college and professional ball. I often felt that playing in thirty-degree weather and in the rain and the snow as the wind blew off the lakes adds toughness to the ballplayers who have to play through those shitty conditions.

After I made the sectional All-Star team as an eleven-year-old, I remember sitting and watching one game from the bench for six innings, stewing because our coach wouldn't start me. I knew I was better than most of the guys, and I couldn't believe that he wouldn't put me in. I was one of the younger guys on the team, and though I knew I was one of the better players, he was almost punishing me because of my age. I was chomping at the bit, because I knew I could make something happen to help the team win. The game went to extra innings, and the coach finally put me in. It reminded me of the scene from *A Christmas Story* when Ralphie, fed up with the bullying, beats the living snot out of Scut Farkus. Something snapped inside of me, and in my own, more productive way, I just wanted to show this guy how wrong he was by not putting me in.

I led off the inning by smacking a double, which led to the winning rally. He put me into the outfield, and I remember being out there all fired up and feeling gratified to realize I had a drive to compete, a drive that I have used to motivate me throughout my career. Even at eleven, I remember thinking to myself, *Don't ever let anyone tell you that you're not good enough.* That was a really big moment, as it helped create the little bit of a chip on my shoulder that I use to motivate myself to this day.

My dad definitely knows the game and loves the sport as much as anyone I've ever met, and he instilled the love of baseball in me at a young age. He taught me a lot about the sport, even though I didn't want to listen. What teenage kid does? We'd battle each other on many car rides home, because I was wound pretty tight during a game and needed time to decompress. Unfortunately for Dad—and likely for anyone who had the displeasure of sitting in the car with us—he wanted to continue coaching long after the final out was made. Even though Dad knows best, I would often challenge him and scream, "Leave me alone!" I just didn't want to hear it.

One story that Dad and I love today, but not so much at the time, was what we affectionately refer to as the "scrapbook story." This argument actually didn't involve pitching, but instead erupted because of my hitting. I was a sucker for the high pitch, and Dad felt the need to weigh in with some hitting advice. As usual, I didn't want to listen and told him he didn't know what he was talking about. Dad grabbed his scrapbook, which was filled with news clippings and stories from his career. He threw it at me and said, "Son, I think I know what I'm talking about." At the time, it was not our greatest moment as father and son, but as I said, we've learned to laugh about it.

Even today, Dad helps me with my game, because he played the game. Though it is a very different game than the baseball he knew, his advice and knowledge of the nuances and the idiosyncrasies of the sport give me a huge advantage in getting through the day-to-day routine. There are so many things that people who have never played the sport don't have a clue about. Having Dad in my corner to lend an ear and give me a shoulder to cry on is absolutely invaluable.

I think what I remember the most was him coming from the Allstate Insurance office at the end of a long work day and driving up to Seneca River North behind the police station in his gray Jetta. I remember that familiar sound of gravel kicking under his tires as he drove across the parking lot. He'd still be dressed in his suit, walking across the field while undoing his tie. Dad didn't give a crap how hot it was or that he was wearing dress clothes; it was time for batting practice. My dad has always been there for me. I can't remember a moment, whether it's a game or just me needing him, when he didn't come through. He never cared about money or anything else; he was just always there. He made sure that every time I fell, he was right behind me to pick me up.

I have my Dad to thank for not only what he taught me about the game, but for the relationship that has evolved between us through baseball. He is the reason I've had so many blessings in my career. He was my jockey, and I was his Seabiscuit. Without him riding my back and teaching me how to compete, I likely never would have gotten into the race at all, let alone be able to enjoy a trip or two to the winners' circle.

Not to be outdone, if you can find a better mother for me on the face of the planet, I'll give up my right arm, which in my case is probably not a very wise thing to do. Mom essentially had to wear the cap of mother and father because Dad was gone much of the time. Now I see my wife and sons experience the same thing when I'm away. I recall a funny moment where the wives of the players were trying to plan a get-together. They decided that a bowling night would be the perfect activity. My mom practically had to bowl with me strapped to her leg, because I had such separation anxiety at the thought of her not being by my side.

When Dad would leave town on long road trips, it was as hard on him as it was on the rest of us, because he was constantly on the go. I know this feeling, now that I have two children of my own. It's the pain in my gut when my son is calling me and asking in his little-boy voice, "Dad, when are you coming home?" I try to get him to understand the concept of ten days, but that is like an eternity for a child. And actually, it's like an eternity for me, too. The trade-off is that I'm able to do an awful lot of fathering and parenting in the time I get with my kids, from morning until midday when I go to work, and then I have four to six months during the off-season to be involved in their lives.

CHAPTER 4

My Incredible Hulk Moment

"*Next to religion, baseball has furnished a greater impact on American life than any other institution.*"

~ Herbert Hoover

I wanted to bottle this feeling and use it as motivation to get me through the rehab process. The night of the injury, while taking refuge at a Best Western near the ballpark, I hopped out of bed with my crutches and literally spent the next twenty minutes hobbling over to the bathroom mirror. My face was drenched with sweat as I placed both hands on the cold white porcelain sink to help me stand. I stared in the mirror and said to myself, "You know what it's going to take to get back. Everyone is counting you out. They think this is your famous final scene—how you're going to leave the game you love." I may even have been counting myself out, but only for a brief moment. I knew I had a big challenge ahead of me, an even bigger challenge than my two elbow surgeries. Not that I would ever want to have Tommy John surgery again, but in some ways, I would've preferred it instead of the surgery and rehab that was in front of me.

At that moment, I looked deep into my eyes and had sort of an out-of-body experience. I felt as though I could see the back of my head, and suddenly, a feeling of peace came over me, as if an angel or God placed his hands upon my nervous soul and reached inside of me to calm my spirit. I knew from that moment that everything was going to be okay. I was confident that I had the drive and the determination to prove everybody wrong. My career was not over, and I knew it. My jersey was essentially ripped from my body, and I was holding on to it for dear life, but I refused to let it go.

I caught my image in the mirror and saw that I had that crazed look one has when he's backed into a corner. It was my David Banner/Incredible Hulk moment. I asked aloud, "How bad do you want this, Grilli? Are you man enough to put in the work to get yourself back?" Of course I was. I had too much to prove to remain in this living hell for as much as another day. I nearly tore the sink from the wall, not with anger, but with a flood of adrenaline and raw emotion, as I was convinced that I was ready to take on the challenge ahead of me. I refused to let that be my last experience putting on a Big League uniform.

The next morning, I went for an MRI so the medical staff could evaluate the severity of the injury. My knee was literally the size of a small pumpkin and felt like it weighed about 500 pounds. It just dangled from my upper thigh, and I truly had a feeling of paralysis. I tried to listen to the conversations of the medical team and gauge the expressions on their faces to gain insight on just how bad the injury might be. They remained poker-faced and spoke in soft tones as they discussed my fate.

Dad flew out to Arizona the moment he learned of my injury. He promised he would stay with me for as long as I needed him. To me, that was even more monumental in my life than when he'd shown up for batting practice in his suit. When you're a kid, you expect your parents to be there each time you fall. You expect them to pick you up, slap a Band-Aid on your knee, and assure you that everything is going to be okay. But I was not a kid anymore, and I was halfway across the country. Yet, without a second thought, my father dropped everything he was doing, packed his bag, and was practically by my side before I was even carried off the field. I only hope and pray that someday I'll be half the father he is.

The morning drive from North Scottsdale to the Goodyear Complex—a drive I once enjoyed taking by myself—took on a different feeling now that my dad was my pro-bono chauffeur, taking me to get treatment before my surgery. Dad eyed me through the rearview mirror while I sat in in the backseat counting cactuses, trying to figure out the reason behind all of this. After weeks of early morning discussions spent trying to make sense of it all, we chalked it up to being a painful chapter of my lifelong story that I can share with my sons someday to teach them how unfair life can seem sometimes.

They say there is a reason for everything that happens in life, but as I lay there with my knee busted up, I couldn't think of a single good one. What doesn't kill you makes you stronger? Well, I thought this might just kill me. All of my hard work flushed down the tubes in an instant. *And for what?* I thought. *For what?* Too often in life I've found myself asking the question, "Why me?"

Don't get me wrong. My life has been far better than many. I'll never lose sight of that, but while lying there with my knee in a cast, my thumb in my mouth, and my future in jeopardy, I thought I was allowed to feel a bit sorry for myself. Since the moment I was chosen in the draft, things have been a bit rocky. I see it as more of a gravel road than the smoothly paved highway to success that I thought it would be, and yet again, I hear the sound of pebbles kicking up under the tires of my baseball life. My career will never be defined as the "smooth-sailing, silver-spooned, sign-for-more-money-than-I-could-ever-count, play-in-the-All-Star-game and get-inducted-into-the-Hall-of-Fame career" that every boy dreams of while lying in his bunk, tossing a ball to the ceiling and watching it drop down into his glove, over, and over, and over again.

The sport isn't an easy one to master, and it gets especially challenging when your ego is checked at the door. I never chased the spotlight that comes along with playing the game. In fact, I lost many good friends by being thrust into the limelight that comes intrinsically with being considered the star of my immediate circle. People became jealous of me when my picture showed up more often than not on the front cover of the sports page in Syracuse. The appearances in the press continued after I went to college. The accompanying relative fame increased with each 1-2-3 inning I threw. People I considered my friends were often jealous, a reaction and emotion that appeared as I grew from little man on the high school campus to big man on the grounds of Seton Hall.

I believed I was entitled to all this favor as part of my plan from God. God and I had many discussions. I did my homework, and I didn't party or experiment with drugs. I always did the right thing. My parents instilled that fear of drugs in me, as well as the fear—or more accurately, the respect—of God in me. I worked too hard to mess things up and to pay the consequences that go hand-in-hand with taking the low road. These same ideals helped make my decision easier when faced with the temptation of taking performance-enhancing drugs to either heal more quickly or escalate my performance. You get one shot at this, and I wasn't going to let my boat sail without me sitting firmly in the passenger seat. I knew that God was the Captain of the ship, and I was glad to be his first mate.

Driving through the Arizona desert with my dad each day felt a bit like the movie *Groundhog Day*. It was incredible how slowly two hours go by when you have nothing to do but think. I swear, if I had recording equipment in my brain, I would have been able to write this entire book during those trips; I relived nearly every moment from birth to the present moment in my mind. When Dad and I ran out of things to talk about, my mind would simply drift as I counted cactuses from Scottsdale to the Indians Spring Training Complex. I stopped counting when I got to about a thousand. Many decisions seem so easy to make when you have the freedom to jump into your car and drive down the road to go here or there. When you must be chauffeured, even the decision to get out of bed is a challenging one. It might just be easier to stay home and suck my thumb, as opposed to having Dad cart my sorry ass to grab one of life's essentials like a burger or a cup of joe.

It was at this time I began journaling on my Blackberry. Those were the notes that have amazingly turned into this book. At the onset, I began journaling simply to keep my mind right during my recovery, but after sharing my rambling thoughts with a few friends, they encouraged me to turn it into the book you are currently reading. I had always planned to put something together to leave as a legacy for my children and a compilation of memories for myself, but I never intended to turn it into book form for the world to see. Lord knows, I had plenty of time to work on this. That's what happens when your world stops on a dime and continues to spin, despite the fact that you are not allowed to participate in it. Minutes seemed like hours. Hours seemed like days.

It became therapeutic for me, though, and I was amazed at how the memories came flooding back to me. I was always afraid of losing the good memories from my career because of the *Groundhog*

Day feeling of playing every day. It makes you take things for granted when you're healthy. Any baseball player's day would be a dream day for most people, but to a ballplayer, every day begins to feel like the day before. It becomes your job if you let it, and soon Sunday seems like Tuesday, and Wednesday seems like Friday. If you didn't have a calendar or the date on the morning newspaper, you'd have no clue what day it was. When you play 162 games and only have eighteen days off, it is very easy to allow that to happen. A different city and a different hotel room every day. A different crowd either cheering for you or shouting obscenities at you. Day after day after day.

So, I decided to journal about my experience in the game, in order to occupy my time and prevent me from pulling out my hair. I was given a gift, and it was important to me to do what I know is in me. I consider myself an artist who was blessed with an amazing skill set, and it is my responsibility to hone my craft to the best of my ability. When you have that gift stripped away from you after you're used to shaping and enhancing it every single day, it can be a very bitter pill to swallow.

Thankfully, I only had to stay in the Best Western close to the field for one night. My Uncle Frank has a beautiful home out in North Scottsdale, Arizona. Up until my injury, my situation couldn't have been better. I stayed in this beautiful palace and I enjoyed my morning commute to and from the park. I spoke to all of my family on the way and made some business calls from my mobile office. Everything was running so smoothly. My gravel road turned to one blocked with boulders in an instant.

My half-decade in the Bigs has been the result of a lot of hard work. Despite wearing labels that were pinned on my back by organizations that thought I wasn't able to get the job done, I think my performance proves otherwise. Everywhere I went, I took the ball, threw strikes, and got people out. Though the wins and losses were not glamorous, my results were consistent. As a late-game reliever, you can throw five solid outings in a row, and then a twenty-five hopper through a drawn-in infield with runners on second and third can send your earned-run average north of five. You really need to be nearly perfect from Opening Day to October to have a glitzy ERA in the role that I perform.

I think about the past two seasons where I was all but run out of the city of Detroit, landed on my feet in Colorado, then jettisoned to Texas, and then had to claw my way off the scrap heap in Cleveland. Yet here I find myself the victim of a blown-out knee, wondering how many more mountains I have to ascend before I am able to feel a sense of relief. Some people have it so easy. Or so we think. Others seem to have the deck stacked against them. Or so we think. I really don't know of many guys who have had to jump hurdles similar to my own in order to get here. Maybe that is a self-centered view and I'm only seeing the world through my jaded sunglasses, but I really feel that lesser men simply quit rather than get up off the mat, dust themselves off, and continue to throw haymakers. I was better than some guys I knew who had blossoming careers, while mine was an uphill battle all the way.

When I was in Detroit, I chased that elusive contract and hated my career more and more. Ending up with the Rockies in 2008 was the best place I could have possibly landed, as it gave me some peace after escaping the Motor City and the boo birds who ran me out of there. I broke down in Texas, after an unexpected early season trade out of Colorado. I'd just about had enough and was so fed up with all the pressures that go along with moving from city to city and getting pushed around and mislabeled, that I began to wonder what it was all for. I was pitching well again after my trade—until I struggled with a bout of tendinitis in my forearm.

People say that if you don't like where you are, then play better.

Well, some people are set up to merely take the fall, while others are destined to succeed. It is kind of like *The Wizard of Oz*. When you get a peek behind the curtain and see what really goes on, there is an "aha" moment—that moment of clarity when you gain life-changing wisdom. I have had my aha moment many times over. I've suffered through three surgeries and have never injected steroids to either heal nor to make me rich. I chose the high road, the path of doing the right thing. I was taught to love and respect the game and wouldn't do anything to tarnish that. I have had to make tough decisions throughout my career and resist the temptation that many others have refused to stay away from. The reward is not worth the risk, and mind you, by *risk*, I don't mean the risk of getting caught or damaging my body, but more importantly, the risk of defaming this amazing game in which I have been blessed to be a part.

I had been in shock for several days after my knee injury, and the reality of it all hit me hard when Dad and I got to Vail. Danielle was home busy with Jayse. She and my parents did not want me alone in Colorado during my surgery so my father flew there to be with me. I hadn't cried since the day the injury occurred, but the shock of looming surgery finally set in. It was as if all the air got sucked from my mid-section. I'd already made up my mind to climb this mountain yet again. I would not leave the game I love like this. I guess the real irony was being geographically positioned at the base of the beautiful Rocky Mountains, while getting pieced back together like a scarecrow. I looked out the window of my room and could not even see the top of the mountains that surrounded me: a virtual real-life metaphor for the climb that lay ahead of me.

It made me reflect on the happy times in my career and on the one time since I entered the league when I felt at peace. Playing for the Rockies for the entire 2008 season and the beginning of 2009 was such a blessing after escaping the whole Detroit Tigers situation.

I loved it there, even though we were so far from my family. It was the perfect place for me to land. The sacrifice was huge, but I had never felt so at ease as when I was a Rockie, but even that didn't last long. Clint Hurdle was my manager there. The relationship that Clint and I formed while I was a Rockie was instrumental in the Pirates making such an effort to snatch me from the Phillies organization in 2011, and I couldn't be more grateful for that. In essence, my time as a Rockie led to the greatest year of my career as a Pirate in 2013.

I'll forever cherish the conversation that Hurdle and I had in the outfield upon my arrival in Denver. During batting practice, he summoned me to the outfield, and as I made my way to short right field, I anticipated the obligatory, "Hey, how you doing? Good to meet you. Did you get in okay, and is your family all right and settled in?" You know, the bit every manager gives upon a new guy's arrival. We talked for what felt like two minutes, and then I expected to be on my way to shag balls pregame before game one as a Rockie, but then he tossed a loaded question toward me. "What do you want out of your career?"

I was shell-shocked. I could not believe that a manager would throw something out there like that right away before getting to know me as a player and a person. The question felt genuine, however, and I thought this was my opportunity to make someone believe I was a valued commodity rather than the way I'd felt just weeks earlier in Detroit when I got booed out of the city I helped get to the 2006 World Series.

Later, Hurdle told me he'd gotten some feedback on me from Leyland and other coaches, but wanted to hear it for himself. Hurdle said that both he and I had the common thread of being first-round picks whose careers hadn't really gone quite as they were scripted. Hurdle asked me what I was in this for, what I wanted to be, and where I wanted this to go.

I took my shot at selling myself to my new organization. I told him that if he really wanted to know, I wanted a chance to work at the back of the bullpen. It's every relief pitcher's dream to be on the mound for the last out of the game. I explained to him that my stats on holding inherited runners from scoring was near the top of the league, but never seemed to be looked at as closely as wins, losses, and ERA. I thought the job I was doing was much harder in the middle of the game, as I faced situations in which I had to make a pitch and clean up a mess I didn't create. Middle relief can be a thankless role, in the same way an offensive lineman is compared to a quarterback or running back. No pitcher ever dreams of becoming a middle reliever, unless they are satisfied with feeling underappreciated or under the radar as just another arm to abuse. If you can get through that and practice surviving those situations, then it can groom you for the pressure of having a clean inning at the end of the game.

I would have remained a Rockie for quite a while, but I defied the Rockies GM when I decided to play in the World Baseball Classic for Italy, and then I chose not to go to "Rockie-fest" due to my son's birthday. Those two choices, which I still believe were the right decisions, rubbed him the wrong way.

My agent at the time—I didn't sign Sheff until the fall of 2011— informed me that I had been labeled a "problem child," and the Rockies management wanted me on the next plane out of town. My punishment for being a malcontent was watching my teammates get a shot at the playoffs in 2009—without me. I really was happy for them, especially considering our bad start. The team got off to a 20-29 start on May 31st before ending 70-43 and finishing as the NL wild-card team. I was proud of them and, admittedly, a bit envious while lying there in a beautiful hospital suite nearly a year later, preparing to be carved like a Thanksgiving bird.

While in Vail, the movie *For Love of the Game* stuck out in my mind. It's a romantic movie, but the parallel seemed a perfect analogy of what I was going through. In the movie, as Kevin Costner is pitching his perfect game, he can't help but think about his career, as a whole, and not about the moment at hand. Even though my situation was not a perfect game, it was in many ways the perfect circumstance to allow me to look back at my career and set me up for what was to come. In that moment when I asked Dr. Steadman, "How likely is my return, Doc?" and he told me it was the worst knee he had ever seen, I was in disbelief. Here I was in the office of a world-renowned orthopedic surgeon at the base of a mountain in Vail, Colorado, where hockey players and football players and skiers go through his operating room like a Ford assembly line, and the knee of a baseball player—my knee—is the worst he has ever seen? Hearing that was gut wrenching and tough to wrap my head around. I looked the doctor in the eye and said, "Look it, just put Humpty Dumpty back together again. Just do your magic, because if you do your thing, then the rest of it is on me."

I couldn't help but lie there and realize that the baseball world does have its perks. Most people who have the misfortune of busting a knee sit in a dark little hospital room in South Podunk and get operated on by a virtual unknown. I, on the other hand, found myself sitting in a luxurious hospital suite with incredible nurses, in arguably the most beautiful spot on Earth, being pieced back together by Dr. J. Richard Steadman. Dr. Steadman added me to his long list of clients whose careers he has saved. In fact, in 2001, Steadman was inducted into the Colorado Ski Hall of Fame for extending the career of so many injured skiers. *Nice frickin' credentials*, I thought. I am so grateful that the Indians organization recognized the severity of my injury and opted to provide me with the greatest care available to the free world. I am sure to this day, that without Steadman, my career would have come to a less-than-spectacular end.

As they wheeled me into the operating room, the bright lights shined on my face. I slid onto the operating table for the fourth time in my life and the third time in my professional career. I was more scared about my arm surgery than I was about this, but this was unnerving due to the complexity of it all. Yet knowing I was in the best place I could have asked for, under the watchful eye of Steadman's staff, put my mind at ease. The Hall of Famer himself pushed me back to his last appointment of the day in order to put his healing hands on me. For sure, the next jersey I put on would go directly to him and join the endless display of memorabilia that graces his walls. I knew I would look back on that day and Steadman would have a big S for *save* on the scorecard next to his name.

CHAPTER 5

LET THE HEALING BEGIN

"The name on the front of the jersey represents who you play for, the name on the back of the jersey represents who raised you. Do them both justice."

~ Baseballisms

My rehab started the following day, and the recovery had been good. Dr. Steadman sat in my room and told me that all went better than he expected. The films didn't show him an accurate diagnosis, but when he got called into the ballgame of surgery, he survived on guts and instincts, and he'd pitched a perfect game. I am eternally grateful. The crowd was going crazy over his success, and my entire support system was so glad it was over.

My adrenaline was running wild because Humpty Dumpty was back together again. I felt so pumped and relieved that the twelve-day waiting period was finally over. The period from March 5th to the 17th, lying there, driving there, waiting for the surgery to take place, was unbearable. Once it was over, I could get on with rehabbing the shit out of it. I had overcome the obstacle. We met the enemy, and we kicked its proverbial ass.

The first day of therapy hit me like a ton of bricks. I tried to prove how tough I was and thought I could outrun my pain medicine. They had me on some pretty good pain meds, and I had a nerve blocker that ran from my groin to my calf. I couldn't feel my leg, and though it felt really heavy, I felt much better than I expected to. It was St. Paddy's Day, and being a quarter Irish, I sat in my room and wolfed down a nice meal of corned beef and cabbage before heading down to do some light therapy. They asked me if I was okay on pain meds, and I advised them that I felt fine and didn't need anything. It was just hours after surgery, and I should have refrained from trying to play the role of Superman.

My nerve blocker wore off, and I couldn't get the medication to catch up fast enough. It was like being kicked square in the balls with steel-toed boots over and over and over again. (Though I've never really experienced that, I think it's a pretty good analogy). The pain radiated through every inch of my body, and I had to keep taking deep breaths to control the pain. People who had come out of surgery the same day were being wheeled through like a NASCAR pit crew changing tires, wheeled in and wheeled out, while I lay on my hospital bed like a cat on the ceiling with his claws out because the pain was so excruciating. The nausea I experienced made it my worst day since the injury, and I prayed to either be healed or die countless times. I actually told the staff to make me suffer for being so stupid. I made this decision, so they should make me pay for it. That's what you get sometimes, being an athlete and thinking you are invincible. I was so mad at myself that I wanted to remember the pain to ensure that I was never that stupid and stubborn again.

My next day of therapy went quite a bit better as my pain medication leveled out. It's amazing how exhausted your body gets from battling not only the trauma, but also the high altitude. I had to make sure I didn't fall face-first off my crutches and I had to learn to maintain control with these two new best friends. It was amazing to see all the people from every corner of the globe who came to this remote town to seek help from the best clinic on the planet. I feel blessed to have the seventy-two-year-old maestro, Dr. Richard Steadman, perform surgery on me.

The rehab clinic was equally incredible. I sat and watched people united by the common bond of their own personal struggles as they coped post-surgery. We formed a tightly knit little group, joined together by an unfortunate set of circumstances, pulling for our own recovery while rooting for each other's healing success.

That day made me really appreciate the feeling of love I have always felt for my father. As a kid, it was throwing batting practice after work. Nearly twenty years later, I sat in a hospital bed while he helped me dress and did nearly everything for me, right down to pulling up my sweat pants and plugging in my cell phone. My father—my best friend, the best man at my wedding, the reason I wore number 49—has always been there for me. We hadn't spent that much time together since I was a little kid. I guess I can count this as a blessing in a sense. My dad didn't think twice about missing work to be with me the entire time I was there. This is yet another reason I hope to be the father to my sons that my father is to me.

We sat there and laughed at the revolving door at the rehab center sitting at the base of the mountain. The hospital is well-positioned for all the wannabe Shaun Whites, as a foot of fresh snow fell to bring on more weekend warriors. I enjoyed skiing as a kid in upstate New York, but sitting there watching repeat customers come through the doors of the hospital, experiencing the pain that I experienced, was something I would not wish on my worst enemy. I guess it is a lesson that is shared and experienced by the inner spirit of many. If you are passionate about living life in your own way and continue to make the sacrifices to do what you love, then sometimes you must experience the pain that comes along with the joy. I just know that after three baseball-related surgeries, I can say I am good. God, grant me five more years of good health, and then I can say I grinded ten major league seasons.

As the sun sat on day two of therapy and rose upon day three, I came to the conclusion that, if oxygen is necessary for healing, then that wasn't the best place to have surgery and recover. We were nearly 12,000 feet above sea level, and there certainly was not an abundance of O_2 floating around up there.

Steadman visited me to start my day, and he gave me another vote of confidence. We made an unscheduled visit to see him again in the rehab clinic, and his facial expressions said it all. He pitched his perfect game on me, and he leaned back and admired his handy work. This was so reassuring after our prior conversation and the looks of confidence we got in our initial meeting with him. "Likely" was the word he initially used when we talked about my comeback, but now it was more like, "Hell, yeah, you're good." My therapist assured me this vote of confidence was saying a lot, coming from the number-one knee surgeon in the world.

Already in my third double-session for the day, my knee was showing signs of minimal improvement. They seemed like huge improvements to me, knowing what it looked like pre-op and then post-op. I looked down at my five-inch incision and imagined that I was outside throwing a football around. The stitching looked just like an NFL ball. The swelling was down and my spirits were up as I progressed to 30 degrees of flexibility and felt like I could climb the mountains that sat outside my bedroom window.

The spirit of the people there was something to be admired. It was inspiring to see the delight on the people's faces going through there. In the other wing of the hospital, those with the pain and misery of fresh injuries had yet to experience the feeling of victory that engulfed the rehab room. They were just beginning their journey and were filled with the fear and trepidation that we all had experienced just a few short days before. But they'll get there. I was confident of that. It is somehow symbolic of life. We are all at different places along the journey of life and here to learn from the experiences of one another.

As the week went by, I experienced another major breakthrough. I was feeling great, as I had been entrenched in the lifestyle and attitude that people took on there. The mountains take hold of you. Even with my leg busted up after surgery, I felt like I wanted to get out there and take on the mountains. Maybe that was the parallel lesson I was learning. I have moved mountains during my life, and God had me resting right in the midst of them as I sat and reflected on the road ahead of me.

The real lesson, however, may be that this was something I needed in order to build character and grow as a human being. I asked myself whether I could live without baseball after experiencing all that was at my disposal as a professional athlete: the sense of entitlement, the money, and the temptation. I am not sure that the average fan can relate to all the pressures, especially for a guy like me who doesn't have a guaranteed contract. To have all that pulled away from me due to one unfortunate misstep during a useless spring-training drill was a big pill to swallow.

I stopped and questioned whether the desire was still burning inside of me, but only for a brief second. You only lose that feeling when you stop trying. I refused to sit back and waste the God-given talent that I had yet to take full advantage of. If Pavarotti was blessed with that incredible, once-in-a-lifetime voice, but had become a grocery-store clerk, the world would've been deprived of an elite talent. The great Gayle Sayers once said, "Motivation without opportunity is a shame, but opportunity without motivation is a waste." You can be sure I took those words to heart and was not going to waste the tremendous opportunity with which I had been blessed.

I continued to journal my recovery, and I entitled that day as "Sometimes you are the pigeon, and sometimes you are the statue." What a day and night I had just survived, though barely. I spent the night mentally wrestling with God, as I was so damn sick of it all. The crutches, my leg brace, the ice machine, and the foot pumps to prevent blood clotting. I had just about reached my breaking point. My mind was racing, and I couldn't go to sleep. As I sank into my bed, ironically in the high altitude, I mined for some bloody chicken cutlets (as Dad and I called them—also known as boogers to most), and watched *Clash of the Titans*. This is one of my favorite flicks and should have made me forget about life for a bit. I lay there, intent on feeling sorry for myself and being frustrated by not being able to play come Opening Day.

Everyone else was supposed to cry for me, but I hadn't allowed myself to cry until that moment. I guess I am human after all. My crutches were sparring with me that morning, and I just about lost it. Trying to get in and out of the shower was a chore, and I had the urge to take my crutches and crack them over my good knee. I guess it is to be expected, but fear, frustration, and self-doubt can become the enemy more than the physical recovery itself.

After my morning therapy session, we were instructed to meet up with Steadman. Going through the back door to his office made me feel like a privileged person. My experience has all too frequently been nothing like that in baseball where we all are herded like cattle. Steadman treated me like a human being, while in baseball we are often made to feel like we are replaceable and are treated like hunks of meat when it comes to the business side of things. Playing Strat-

O-Matic Baseball with real people shouldn't be how things are done, but most times, it feels like you are treated like a commodity and not a person.

Though the Indians did the right thing by sending me there, they did throw up some roadblocks and conducted business as I expected them to. They questioned Steadman's protocol to keep me there until Friday and lobbied to have me go back to Goodyear to get treatment from their staff, at a savings to their budget, of course. Then they had lined up only one therapy session per week, which is totally ludicrous. I persisted in order to get what I wanted, which was a five-day-per-week therapy regimen at Melissa Brown PT and Sports Medicine. Behind the scenes, all the horses are fed, but some of them aren't fed the good quality apples. I just had to go and get my own apples. It wasn't the first time I'd have to find a way to feed myself.

Then the news I'd been expecting became official. While enjoying a nice dinner at La Bottega Italian, we were interrupted by a call from my agent, Mike Moline. It's ironic that the restaurant's advertising slogan is *"Celebrando La Vita,"* which translates to celebrate life. In the midst of trying to down another bite of eggplant parmesan, my *celebrando* was interrupted. It came as no surprise to me, but Moline informed me that the Indians placed me on the AAA disabled list for the entire year.

CHAPTER 6

A Slice of Life in the Minor Leagues

> *"We lost fourteen games in a row. Then we had a game rained out. It felt so good we had a victory dinner."*
>
> ~ Lefty Grove as a minor-league manager

Looking back, I never had a silver spoon up my butt like most first-round picks. Sure, I signed for some great money, but I earned it, worked hard, and didn't test the system. I played by the rules and didn't pull any J.D. Drew/ Scott Boras shady shit. Boras advised Drew not to accept the Philadelphia Phillies' $3 million offer, and instead, he had Drew sign a professional contract with the independent St. Paul Saints. Boras and the players association then filed a grievance to have Drew declared a free agent since only "amateurs" could be subject to the amateur draft. Boras won the argument, but the arbitrator ruled he could not grant Drew free agency since he was not a member of the Players Association. Instead, Drew re-entered the draft the following year and signed with the St. Louis Cardinals for nearly three times the Phillies' best offer. It should have come as no surprise, but Drew was booed as loudly as Santa Claus every time he stepped foot in Philly.

I signed with the Giants for $1.875 million dollars, and being a small town guy from Baldwinsville, New York, I didn't know how people were going to respond to that kind of money. I was scared they knew where I lived and were going to start egging the house, or start calling me to ask for money. I didn't realize how much money that actually was, and I was just excited that I may finally be able to buy my own car. I had driven rust buckets through high school. A family friend, Tom Keane, used to let me use his old clunker of a green pick-up that had an AM radio in it and a piece of plywood so you wouldn't fall through the rusty floor. I could see the road under my feet through holes next to the wood. I just tried to keep it real, and even when I played A ball out in San Jose, I had this old car that sounded like a bi-plane provided by the host family. Even though I had money at that time, I didn't want to flaunt it in front of the guys who hadn't signed for as much as I had.

When I signed, I initially bought two things in Syracuse: a 1998 Land Cruiser, paid for in cash, and a black leather jacket that I thought made me look like a badass. I thought I was smart for buying the Land Cruiser instead of a hot rod in which I could only fit a small suitcase, because I knew I would be headed out West and I could throw all my belongings in the back of the Land Cruiser and head out across the country. Prior to receiving my bonus, I thought the hundred dollars I earned working for my dad's bar was a lot of money. That was until I wrote a check to the IRS that had so many zeroes, it made my hand tremble. At the recommendation of my Uncle Frank, I made some good investments with the rest to let my money work for me. You hear about so many guys who piss away their money, and I didn't want to be one of them. I didn't need much, so it made more sense to put my signing bonus away and forget about it.

In some ways, I wished I was in the '98 draft, because I may have gotten a more lucrative contract due to the way business was handled after the J.D. Drew process. I didn't want to delay my dream of playing in the Bigs any longer. I wanted to get my career moving forward and not just feel like I was trying to win the lottery. I loved the game, respected it, and I still do. I was going to work harder to reach my dream and make my mark in baseball history.

My projection was high, as I was a big-time prospect starting out. All the others around me had prospered far better than I had, and I seemed to have missed out on something along the way. It seemed that while most of the guys in my draft class were treated as the grand marshals in the parade to the major leagues, I was left to sweep up after the elephants. I was adapting and trying to succeed in every situation I was put into. I did well and did what was asked of me, and yet I never seemed to catch a break.

After games, a lot of the guys would go out and drink beer, but I still wasn't old enough and had a shitty fake ID, so even trying to fit in with the rest of the team and become one of the guys was a challenge. Between waking up each morning on the other side of the country, eating meals at fast-food restaurants, taking eight-hour bus rides to games in the hot California heat, and being the victim of a house mom vixen, I'd had just about enough of A ball.

One of the cooler guys on the team was Kevin Rogers, who was almost twenty-nine years old at the time and trying to recover from a blood clot in his arm, an injury that ultimately ended his career. Rogers, who was a left-hander with a funky delivery, took teammate Scott Linebrink and me under his wing. He made sure we were comfortable on the bus and protected us a bit from some of the rookie hazing that most guys have to endure. I was actually skinny enough that I could sprawl out in the overhead compartments of the bus with a pillow, instead of being all scrunched into a seat, which made the eight-hour bus rides to some places a bit more tolerable.

I was also teammates with Bobby Bonds, Jr., Barry's younger brother, whose locker was right next to mine. I guess he saw me as the golden boy, and he tried to hit me up for money from the day I walked into the locker room. "Yo, man, loan me a hundred grand, and I'll flip it."

Every day he'd tell me why he needed a hundred grand, until I finally said, "Bobby, I don't understand why you're asking me for money. Your brother Barry has got more money than I'll ever sniff. Why don't you borrow it from him?" I stuffed a 100 Grand candy bar and a contract into an envelope, and the requests subsided. I was learning quickly how to adjust to the nuances of life in the game, something I may not have been able to handle had I signed when I was seventeen.

When I walked in for the first time with my bag slung over my shoulder, Bobby and some of the other guys gave me the hairy eyeball as I made my way into the locker room. I could hear some of the Latin players referring to me as the guy with the golden spikes, but I *todo comprendo* what they were saying, the result of four years of high school *Español*. They soon learned that I put my pants on the same way they did and didn't expect any preferential treatment. It wasn't long before they accepted me as one of their amigos.

Unfortunately, I signed late, and though I could practice with the team and take the long rides to away games, I couldn't play for the team. This is another way the team keeps you under control for an extra year so you don't use up a year of service time. I spent the games up in the stands charting pitches and scouting without ever being able to suit up for a game or step on the field.

After the minor-league season ended, I was sent off to Instructional League in Scottsdale, where we played long hours of baseball in the hot desert sun and stayed three to a room in a dilapidated roach motel that used to be a Best Western. They served us hot soup and crackers for lunch, and we had to use our own money to buy candy bars from the snack bar to give us enough energy to make it through the day. Some of the guys would take an entire sleeve of crackers to try to fill their bellies so they could last until supper time. Those of us who had some money would head down to the mall after practice and crush some fast food from the food court before heading back, taking a nap, and hustling down to dinner, before partying like a rock star at night. Such is the glamorous life of the minor league ballplayer.

My summer of Instructional League miraculously was cut short. Mike Glendenning, Damon Minor, Giuseppe Chiaramonte, and I were all shipped off to the lovely island of Oahu to the Hawaiian League. How lucky am I, having traveled to Italy, San Jose, Arizona, and Hawaii to not only play the game I love, but to get paid for it. As often as I may have complained about the squalid conditions and the challenging host families, I was really enjoying this life and I wouldn't have traded it for anything.

We joined an outstanding team called the Honolulu Sharks who played their home games at the University of Hawaii. We were once again robbed of our personal space as four of us had to share a one-bedroom apartment. The original plan was for Chiaramonte and me to split an apartment and for the other two guys to do the same. When we got there, we learned that Minor and Glendenning had made the trip with only a couple hundred bucks in their pockets and no credit cards. Chiaramonte and I had signed for quite a bit more than the other two, so being the kindhearted souls that we were, we diced up our apartment into fours so our teammates would have a place to bunk. Our apartment wasn't in the greatest of neighborhoods, and though they have since cleaned it up, there were a lot of bars, prostitutes, and gender-benders who set up shop in the area. Needless to say, we were careful where we ventured off to at night.

There were only four teams in the league, but we were able to see several of the different islands during our time there, and we actually went on to win the Hawaiian League Championship. Though not the World Series, it was still an outstanding feeling to win at any level and winning in my first pro-ball experience was especially sweet. Though we didn't win a World Series ring, we did win a Hawaiian League watch, and it gave me a taste of what it felt like to win.

During a meaningless game toward the end of the season, the grounds crew had the seventh game of the World Series between the Marlins and the Indians on TV, and a bunch of us kept sneaking into the maintenance shack to keep an eye on the game.

Our manager, Dave Anderson, came in and ripped into us. "Hey, get out of there. We got a game to win here." We went back into the dugout, but kept sneaking back to catch the score because the game was so intense, and we were all so far away from home that, at that moment, watching the World Series seemed far more important than winning a nothing game in October in the Hawaiian League.

From the beautiful Hawaiian Islands, I climbed another rung on the ladder and was shipped off to Double-A in Shreveport, Louisiana, of the Texas League. I broke my streak of living with possessed host families and roomed with McKinley, who was my buffer back in San Jose. We both had a bit of cheese put away and decided to rent a nice apartment and some furniture, so we were living large and not living stupid.

The bus rides were ridiculously long in the Texas League, and the air was so thick you could practically cut it with a knife. Oftentimes, the bus would leave just after midnight to get to an afternoon game the next day. Linebrink used to buy a swimming pool flotation device and lay it in the bus aisle so he'd have a quasi-air mattress to sleep on. Such was the life of the minor leaguer.

I remember one game that I lost was called after five innings because of a tornado warning. We were up 2-0 against the Jacksonville Generals, and I had thrown a no-hitter for four-and-two-thirds innings. As the storm was rolling in, I felt myself getting a bit out of sync as I felt that they were going to start pulling the tarps, and I wanted to get out of the inning so it would be an official game. The next guy spanked a single into left to break up the no-hitter, then I walked a guy, and then—like a scene from *The Natural*—Duane Ward hit a three-run bomb just as sirens started blaring. The skies opened up, and it started to rain buckets and hail. I ran into the dugout just ahead of the storm. I was so pissed off to lose the game in such a fashion. Linebrink started laughing at how quickly things unraveled, and I literally wanted to knock him out, because I was so pissed at how I'd lost the game.

Aside from that, it was a memorable season playing in Louisiana. The clubhouse was too small and the bus rides too long, but the memories will never leave me. I remember stopping by the side of the road at an old filling station that had been turned into a mudbug station. They had dirty coolers filled with crawfish, and they would scoop crawfish, a few spicy Cajun-style potatoes, and an ear of sweet corn into a plastic grocery bag. We brought our lunch into the clubhouse, which was so hot and smelled so bad already that the stink of crawfish actually enhanced the odor.

Later that season, I made the Double-A All-Star team, but I didn't get to play in the game because I pitched just before the break. Soon after that, I was called up to Triple-A Fresno, which I truly felt was a bit too quick. Here I was in my first year of pro ball, and I had already made it to Triple-A. I didn't feel like I was entirely ready for all of that, and I wished that my meteoric rise through the system would slow long enough for me to catch my breath and develop at a more realistic pace. Mentally, it's a process that you need to go through in order to be mature enough to face Big League hitters. I felt like I had gotten thrown into the whirlwind and without time to process what was happening.

CHAPTER 7

FRESNO TO CALGARY TO FLORIDA VIA OMAHA

> "Like all great travelers, I have seen more than I remember, and remember more than I have seen."
>
> ~ Benjamin Disraeli

The whirlwind Jason Grilli baseball extravaganza tour made its next stop in Fresno, where I went at a speed of 110 mph face-first into the proverbial wall. It was a challenge for a number of reasons, and the game suddenly became difficult for me. I needed to learn to deal with professional hitters, and that was a tall order for a twenty-year-old who only had been playing professional ball for a year.

To complicate things, we didn't have our own ballpark, as the new downtown stadium for the Fresno Grizzlies hadn't been completed, and we had to play our home games at Fresno State. The stadium was like an airport, where any ball hit toward the Corona Pavilion in right field would take off like a missile. This resulted in our team having three of the league leaders in the Pacific Coast League (PCL) in home runs allowed. Unfortunately, I was number three, finishing the season with twenty-nine gopher balls surrendered. It wasn't uncommon to give up a seven spot in two or three innings' work and leave the game feeling as if you'd just had your ass handed to you.

To compound things, the PCL is known as a hitter-friendly league since many of the stadiums were built at a high altitude. I remember facing David Ortiz, who was then in the Twins organization and playing in Salt Lake City. He hit a change-up off me that still hasn't landed. If you look at the batting averages of players who played in the PCL, they are often through the roof, and earned run averages naturally reside right up there with them.

I pitched scared most of the season as my confidence wavered, and it seemed as though my breaking ball really deserted me. At one point, our pitching coach tried to change my mechanics and told me I should try pitching like Kerry Wood. I had always tried to be coachable and to take the advice of those who know the game better than I did, but I never understood why someone would try to change my entire approach to pitching.

Socially, there were a lot of older guys on the team who were on the downward track and were trying to hold onto their baseball lives. The locker room can be filled with a bunch of Bitter Bobs who not only refuse to relate to the younger guys, but cast a negative cloud over the team. It seemed like the guys would knock over spread tables, take themselves out of the lineup, or argue amongst each other on an every-other-day basis. That tends to be the case often in Triple-A, where everyone is so close to the Bigs, and yet so far away. Every time the phone rings, each player thinks it's his turn, which creates an atmosphere of competition and jealousy unlike other levels.

Because we were in a temporary ballpark, we didn't even have our own clubhouse, but instead showered and changed after each game in a trailer that they turned into a makeshift locker room behind the right field wall. To be confined in those tight quarters with a group of guys who really didn't want to be there drove me to the point that I asked our manager, Ron Roenicke, if he could arrange to have me sent back down to Double-A, because it was so much more enjoyable.

At that point, baseball had become a job to me, and I dreaded it each time I turned the doorknob and walked into the clubhouse. Baseball had always been fun for me, but suddenly it had transformed into an eight-to-five, where I felt like I was punching the clock and waiting for quitting time. I ended the season at 8-10 with an ERA north of six, and I wondered if I was ever going to get it together again.

It was May 11, 2000, the anniversary of my Big League debut, and Danielle and I found out about getting the call up to the majors while I was playing in Calgary. Yes, Calgary, home of the Florida Marlins' AAA farm club. I hated both the daily life and playing baseball in that miserable place.

I had been traded from Fresno during a road trip in a deal that sent Liván Hernández, a World Series MVP, to the Giants, and Nate Bump, a pitcher from Penn State, and me to the Marlins. I got a phone call from Bobby Evans, who was the traveling secretary for the Giants at the time. I thought my teammates were playing a trick on me, as it really did not sound like him on the phone. Bobby took a deep breath into the phone, and I could tell he was a bit on edge at having to break the news to me. After hanging out late the night before with teammates Mike McMullen and Joe Nathan, I was sleeping late, because there was nothing to do at the Red Lion in Omaha, Nebraska, short of experiencing some fine dining at your local Waffle House. I turned on the TV, and at the bottom of the screen on ESPN, a ticker came across as I processed all this, and I realized it was no joke. I went across the hall and told McMullen and Nathan, who in turn thought that I was screwing with them.

I learned very early that this was a business, and I was merely a commodity. Despite my signing bonus, I was not indispensable. I could be shipped out without them giving it a second thought. I was merely a chip, and with one of me, they could get one of him, and such is the business of baseball. Like many jobs, the worker is far more committed to the company than the company is to the worker. The sooner I learned that, the easier it would be for me.

Getting traded to the Florida Marlins seemed appealing on paper—until I realized that baseball's southern-most team houses their Triple-A team in North America's northern-most baseball city, Calgary, Alberta, Canada. I couldn't even believe that baseball existed there. I found myself suffering mild depression that set in as I walked into the old, run-down ballpark that the Cannons called home. The place was a dump. History would soon prove that when the Cannons moved to Albuquerque several years later, it was because of the dump that was their home. Foothills Stadium had the smallest clubhouses known to man, and we *maybe* drew about thirty-two fans when it was $1 beer night. This was the land of hockey and dog sleds, and I was sentenced to doing time in Calgary, Alberta, of all places. It may as well have been Siberia. The city itself was decent to be in, but to play baseball in that God-awful part of the world felt like I had fallen completely off the map. To put it in perspective for non-geography majors, Calgary is situated four hours north of Montana and is 700 miles closer to Juneau, Alaska, than it is to Toronto. It wasn't the end of the earth, but you could certainly see it from there.

As if that wasn't bad enough, it was the heyday of the steroid era and the first time I had witnessed needles being passed around the locker room. I sensed that part of the reason was that guys wanted to get out of that God-forsaken part of the world so badly they would resort to cheating to escape. It was another ugly side of the game that I hoped never to witness, but I'd be lying if I said that I didn't contemplate joining the ranks of the users as well. I was pitching poorly, hated the place, and understood in some small way why players chose to stick themselves in the ass, rather than spend another night in Calgary. True to my beliefs and true to the game I love, I resisted temptation and chose to do my time on the PCL's version of death row.

Waiting for a call-up to Florida would require a ton of patience and some major adjustments to the ego, not to mention a 3000-mile plane ride. I remember walking every day into the clubhouse and seeing the flag not just blowing straight out and at full attention, but it was actually blowing up—skyward. At times, I'd look at the flag, which was Canadian, I might add, and it looked like it were frozen solid. Not fun for a pitcher's confidence before even throwing his first pitch.

I was so happy to have been drafted by the Giants, and I thought I would make my debut just a few years later in the new ballpark by the bay. I even took a tour of the grounds when the building phase was going on so I could acclimate to the city of San Francisco. Little did I know that I would ultimately pitch there, but as the opposition, instead of as a Giant. Ironically, I got my first career save there as a member of the Rockies in 2008.

At that time, I was a Cannon and a member of the Marlins organization, and I had to hang my hat in my new home. Things started out fine. As in my first outing, I pitched as if I knew I did not want to be there any longer than necessary. I threw six no-hit innings right out of the gate. I felt like this was going to be a temporary layover and that I was seasoned enough to get my shot to break into the Bigs sooner, rather than later. My over-inflated sense of optimism kept me sane for a while, until my ERA ballooned to around 6.5 after a couple of bad outings.

One day, out of nowhere, the clouds miraculously parted, and the sunshine broke through the overcast Calgary skyline. There were two injuries in the Marlins rotation, and I was summoned to the Big Leagues. Oddly enough, it was not just one starter, but two who got bit by the injury bug: Alex Fernandez, who went down for the Marlins, and Ricky Bones, the team's spot starter and long reliever. It was my turn in the rotation, but instead of toeing the rubber in Calgary, I would be taking the hill as a Marlin.

Prior to that day, my arm had been popping to the point that it sounded like I was cracking my knuckles. It got progressively worse over time, but I figured it was either from the cold weather or just the normal, everyday grind that I signed up for and was part of being a pitcher. It was a rite of passage, of sorts, to have a bum elbow, shoulder, or both when you make the decision to throw a baseball for a living, the most unnatural thing you can ever do to your joints and ligaments. Think of the stress and strain you are asking the body to undergo by taking an object that weighs only five ounces and throwing it at speeds of over 90 mph. It's no wonder your elbow doesn't fly from your bicep, a la Dave Dravecky, with each and every throw.

My father even kept asking me how my arm felt, and I kept telling him that it felt good, but some days it felt like I was working harder than usual. My velocity indicated that something wasn't 100 percent right. I would throw one heater at 94, then another fastball would come in at 87. I think the coaches equated that to my sinker versus four-seamer instead of an indication that something was happening within my arm.

I needed to push that aside, as I would soon find myself throwing high heat at the lineup of the big, bad Braves. I felt excited, but pissed off that my performance was not the reason I got called at that point. More so, it was just my turn to pitch in the rotation. I somehow envisioned that my call to the majors would be by destiny and not by default. No matter what, I was getting my chance, and I was not going to let it turn to shit.

During the long flight from northwest Canada to the southeast U.S., I remember making notes of all the baseball fields scattered across the landscape, which I looked down upon from miles up in the sky. I reflected on the dream I had fulfilled and the journey I had taken to get me where I was going that day. I pressed my forehead against the cold window, and I couldn't help but think back to where it all began: in my backyard in upstate New York.

Nearly a dozen years later, the realization of my dream was finally coming true. The stewardess tapped me on the shoulder, waking me from my daydream to offer me a Coke and a bag of nuts. I accepted, and I immediately got a nervous feeling in the pit of my gut as I snapped back into the present moment. From the second a player is drafted, from the minute he gets that long-awaited phone call, his life changes. It's the best feeling in the world, knowing you are being recognized for the hard work you have put in up to that point. There really is no amount of money that can replicate that moment you realize you do something so many people dream about, but few get to experience. And there I was, headed to Miami to face a major league lineup that included the likes of Chipper Jones and Andruw Jones, Andrés Galarraga, Brian Jordan, Bobby Bonilla, and Javy López. These were the baseball cards every kid had stored in an overflowing shoebox, and there I would be, facing this modern-day Murderers' Row. I wanted to make my mark. I wanted to stand out in the eyes of the front office.

I took that moment to understand this was not to be a one-shot deal for me. Even though they told me it was a spot start and I was only going up for one day, it was one day I would never forget. As irony would have it, the date of my first Major League Baseball win was May 11, 2000, the same day my father earned his initial win as a member of the Detroit Tigers twenty-five years earlier.

I was taking on the Braves, the team that had dominated the National League for several decades. Kevin Millwood was my nemesis that day, coming off a season in which he'd been an All-Star and had come in third place in the Cy Young balloting. Their lineup was stacked top to bottom with so many great-caliber ballplayers, and there I was, still damp behind the ears, making my debut. My expectation to just make pitches calmed my nerves, and I was not going to get caught up in the moment. *Make my pitches, throw strikes, make my pitches, throw strikes.*

Paul Bako was my Big League catcher that day, a third-year player who would ultimately get traded to the Braves later that season. He was great; he kept me cool, calm, and collected. I made pitches and hoped for the best. I trusted my teammates. Mike Lowell was a great teammate and was pumping me up the whole time. I felt as though these guys had my back, despite the fact that I was a newbie. For them, it was a big game to set the tone for a mid-summer run. A game to show you what kind of team you have going into the dog days of summer.

Expecting a rookie to step in and win his Big League debut against a star-studded lineup was pretty unlikely, but I didn't care what everyone else thought. I had my own agenda when it came to silencing the naysayers.

As I went over the scouting report, I thought it was a joke. It said that hitters were unable to hit the curveball down, and make sure you move their feet. I had known that since Little League. This was nothing new or innovative. I trusted that Bako and I would get on the same page, and I would pay attention and try to figure out hitters' swings as best as I could. I felt it was better to stick to my strength rather than to sell out to a player's weaknesses. Hell, they'd never faced me before, either, so it was the battle of the unknowns, and I hoped to come out on top.

Whatever I did worked, because I came through with my first Big League win, first major league hit, and drove in the winning RBI. I wasn't lights out, but lasted six and two-thirds, gave up eleven hits, struck out three, and hit two batters, but came through with a "W." What a night!

The downside of it all was after the game, when they told me I was only making one start and was headed back to the Great White North in Calgary. The team celebrated with me for only a minute, because they were heading to NYC to face the Mets. I was there enjoying my cold beer and even got my father to come into the locker room to celebrate with me. It was anticlimactic in the sense that my night of success had an element of buzz kill. I knew at that moment I was being shipped back to Calgary!

I was again a Cannon before my locker even knew I was gone. My return was followed by the worst bullpen session of my life. The team was back in Portland, Oregon, and I felt like all the adrenaline from my cameo appearance as a Big Leaguer was sucked right out of me. It was time to get back into my five-day routine of in-between starts.

Little did I expect that my arm would respond in a way that had me in tears, afraid something major was wrong. I had to abort my bullpen session because I could barely get the ball to the plate. I must have been hitting the gun at 70 mph tops, and if there was a pane of glass between me and home plate, the ball would have bounced back at me. The shooting pain that came over me was so freaking scary, I nearly cried!

I stopped the pen session and headed directly to the training room. It was there that I spotted Joe Strong, a teammate who happened to be in the bathroom area. Strong was a story himself and a portrait of living out a dream, no matter how many obstacles he faced, no matter where he had to go or how long it took him to get the call to the Bigs. Strong had attended the University of California, Riverside, where he was drafted by the Oakland Athletics in the fifteenth round in 1984. When the players went on strike eleven years later in 1995, Strong was a replacement player and was therefore banned from joining the Major League Baseball Players Association. He was released by the Chicago Cubs organization in 1995 and played independent ball for a while, before dropping out of ball altogether for two seasons. He came back, played in Korea, and ultimately played in five countries during a sixteen-year career. He finally made his major league debut for the Marlins the same night I made mine on May 11, 2000. It was ironic that my career path was marked with perseverance, and yet it paled in comparison to his. His debut made him the oldest major-league rookie since 1960 at nearly thirty-eight years old. Much like me, he made one appearance and shuffled back on the slow train to Calgary.

I sat down on a bench near the showers to collect my thoughts and regroup. I just had a career highlight, and now I was paying the price, which would delay any hope of my return back to the show. *This can't be happening*, I thought. I had good mechanics and felt like I was above getting injured. I found out rather quickly that I am not Superman and that this was part of the game. I was sent to see the orthopedic doctor down in San Francisco, who told me that I had an inflamed ligament, but no stress fracture or anything from which I couldn't bounce back. Just the same, it was my first experience facing my own pitching mortality.

The team sent me to Melbourne, Florida, to do some rehab. I tried so hard to figure out how I was going to get through the pain.

The team shut me down to see if time off was what my arm needed, before I started up again a few weeks later on a throwing program. I saw the team doctors in Miami several times, who put me through all kinds of tests. There were no indications from doctors or from regular X-rays that there was any cause for alarm. After a few weeks of rest, followed by some light throwing and then another visit or two to the trainers, I realized that I was just increasing my pain tolerance at the expense of delaying the inevitable.

After the team doctors admitted they weren't quite sure what was wrong, I demanded a second opinion. A team doctor suggested that I go see renowned surgeon Dr. James Andrews. Both the team doctor and one of Andrews' understudies came clean, after all those weeks of head scratching, and said they believed that I had a broken arm or stress fracture. I could see clear as day when they put the film over the light that there was a pencil-line fracture through the olecranon bone. I nearly lost it when they told me this.

"You mean to tell me that a simple X-ray shows that I had this going on the entire time, and no one picked up on it?"

He said, "Well, that is what I see, but let Dr. Andrews give you his professional opinion." I was so pissed that tears of rage filled my eyes, and I grabbed the training table I was sitting on and pushed it over. The emotion of not being able to pitch anytime soon gripped me and caused me to flip out.

Upon seeing Dr. Andrews, I was informed that my stress fracture was so bad that it now required a pin the size of my pinky to be inserted in my olecranon bone, which is the curvy bone that sits right behind the elbow. Dr. Andrews went on to drop the anvil on me when he told me that he most likely would see me within a year or two to do a Tommy John surgery.

I could not comprehend this at the moment. I had just made my MLB debut, and not a month later, I nearly regurgitated in my mouth when I learned my career could be over. I felt like Archibald Moonlight Graham in *Field of Dreams*. One and done. I sipped from a cup of coffee and spilt the damn thing all over the front of my uniform right after the game.

Two months later, in August, I found myself dressed in a hospital gown, being wheeled down the hospital corridor about to go under the knife for the first time. The only positive thing I could glean was peace of mind in knowing that I was under the care of Andrews, who is well-known for his mastery of putting many athletes back together.

It gave me peace as I looked around his office at all the jerseys and signed pictures and memorabilia expressing the sheer gratitude of all those who had gone to Dr. Andrews before me.

I told myself that I'd missed too much time already, and a potential call-up in September was not going to happen this year. Since I was near home and in a HealthSouth facility, I began to rehab hard for the next four months and planned to make 2001 my coming-out party. I was not going to miss another day, and I needed to get back to where I wanted to be.

I received an invitation to Marlin Fest before the start of the 2001 season. I had worked my ass off both in the rehab room and at the gym, and I'd hired Randy Hadley, a renowned personal trainer, to help get me in shape to combat the steroid junkies who littered the road in front of me. I also used the time to take some college courses to chip away at earning a degree, a promise I had made to my mother upon signing.

I threw a bullpen session just four months after surgery in the presence of the front office and some coaches. With the exception of one coach (who will remain nameless), they were very positive and optimistic at my progress and acknowledged that I had worked my tail off. To this day, I love when people doubt I can do something. I use it to fuel my fire, so in some ways, I tip my cap to nameless coach. As Mark Twain once said, "It is better to remain silent and be thought a fool than to open one's mouth and remove all doubt."

It was expressed to me, however, that I should not expect to make the team. I told management to not count me out, and I looked right through the man who tried to deflate me. To their surprise, I made the team. I knew I was not at my best, only flipping up 87-90 mph fastballs with less stuff than normal, but apparently I was good enough to solidify a spot on the Marlins' opening-day roster, a beautiful, sunshiny 3000 miles away from Calgary.

CHAPTER 8

HEAVEN IS MISSING AN ANGEL

"It makes me want to cry when people tell me I am an inspiration to them. I never knew there were so many wonderful people out there."

~ Bree McMahon

A week had passed since my surgery, and my progress continued. My knee was cranked up to 40 degrees of motion, and all systems were go. It was a lazy day, and Dad and I couldn't wait to get home. The weather was cold, so we couldn't do much except chill and wonder what was to come next. The end of our time together was nearly upon us. We both sat without saying a word to each other and reflected on the unplanned father/son time we'd enjoyed during the unexpected adventure. It was a far cry from playing catch on the end of Walpole Lane, but it had been a different type of "field of dreams" for us. Silence engulfed the two of us for the moment, but I knew we were sharing the same thoughts. It had been an absolute treat to be with my father, an unexpected by-product of a series of unfortunate events. He had been instrumental in all the positive moments in my life, and I am so grateful. It was nice to see him rest for a change, since he normally goes 110 miles an hour to provide for my mom and himself.

I had an appointment at nine o'clock, and we hung back for a while to see Dr. Steadman. Once again, he gave me a great progress report and the protocol to strictly follow until I returned six weeks later. I gave him a firm handshake to thank him once again, but I also felt compelled to hug the genius. So I did. I was fighting back tears while I thanked the man who saved my career. As I walked away, I sensed that the doc was looking at me, knowing he'd done a good job of putting me back together. I knew he'd sneak a peek at the box scores over the next few seasons and subliminally take a little credit whenever he saw me take the ball.

Dad and I then went to the Westside Cafe to grab breakfast. We heard nothing but rave reviews about the Captain Crunch French Toast: "French bread dipped in our special batter, then dredged in crushed Captain Crunch and griddle-fried golden brown." It lived up to all expectations. We then went back for therapy session number two, before venturing over to Lionshead Village to take the gondola to the very top of Vail Mountain. I was bursting with a Rocky Balboa feeling, excited to see how high the mountaintops actually are. The journey to the peak made me refocus on what lay ahead on the difficult road.

I was as close to God as I had ever been at that very moment. I knew His purpose was buried somewhere in the adventure. I'd just had a successful surgery, and I was standing with my father on top of a mountain in Vail. We went to have a quick beer at the top, before returning to the bottom to complete our day at Montauk Seafood Restaurant. It was a great way to finish my time with Dad. We watched as Syracuse blew the NCAA tournament, losing to Butler in the Sweet Sixteen, and I couldn't remember when Dad and I were last able to share that kind of time. We never even talked about baseball; we just enjoyed each other's company. I told him often how much I appreciated all he had done for me, taking three weeks off to be away from home and his business without even giving it a second thought.

Dad, I aspire to be such a great family man.

It was our last night there, and we were both very excited to be taking a flight back to Orlando to see Jayse and Danielle. That would be the best medicine I could ever ask for. I have continually drawn from the positives instead of the negatives. I have witnessed sick hospitals, children with disabilities, and kids with disfigurements, all seemingly placed before me to help me understand that my problems are not so bad. God will place things before you to awaken the soul, to make you realize that things aren't so bad. "Sleep well, Cheese. Your mind is positive and rejuvenated, because you are strong when the mind is strong." Maybe that is the lesson in all of this.

The sun set and rose yet again, and it felt like an eternity to get to that day. It was the last day for Dad and me to spend some quality time together in Vail. We had an early appointment to squeeze in, and then said goodbye to a very magical place where good people give all their heart and soul and every ounce of sweat and toil to help patients get healthy again. Everyone—from the doctors to the physical therapists to the people we met from all over the world— worked diligently to make it a happy place to be. Maybe it really is true that misery loves company.

Thank God we left when we did to head back to Denver, since the storms were coming in again, and we saw cars spinning off the road, one after the other. We made it through the pass, only to find out that our flight had been cancelled. Yet another speed bump on our long and winding road. We got booked on the next flight and were seated in first class after getting groped, frisked, fondled, and manhandled like a scene from *Meet the Parents* with me playing the role of Gaylord Focker. I was annoyed again to find myself trapped in such a situation, but I kept telling myself to roll with it and have patience.

Dad and I had a great flight home, despite my inability to keep my leg bent comfortably so it could fit under the first-class seat. We had a great conversation and finished off the trip with another couple of hours of wonderful father/son chat. Many times in life, we look back and wish we had spent more time with our parents, time we can't get back but wish that we could. I feel confident that I'll look back on those few weeks and have no regrets, and though our "field of dreams" took place in a rehab facility instead of a cornfield, I know we had one hell of a catch.

Returning home was a blessing from the Good Lord above. Hugging Danielle and throwing Jayse up on my shoulders was the best medicine I could have ever asked for. You realize how important family really is when the chips are down. They never leave you when things like this happen, or at least that has been my experience, and I'm thankful for that. Jayse stayed up the night we got home. After he saw Daddy and Grandpa, he just couldn't settle back down. He was a little uneasy and unsure, seeing my new equipment clanging through the house. As open as our home is, I quickly figured out that my crutches would be a hindrance, no matter where I tried to go. My bed never felt better, especially with Danielle finally lying by my side.

Small victories had been won, and I finally got my stitches out. I'm amazed that I didn't go all Hulk and rip them out myself before then, but somehow I showed restraint.

While at therapy, I met an amazing young girl named Bree McMahon, who was put into my life to help me put my issues in perspective. Bree had been the victim of a bad accident that had taken one of her legs and nearly cost her a soccer scholarship, which the school ultimately still gave to her. As I sat on the training table going through my series of exercises, I started feeling sorry for myself, because I was having a horse-shit day. I pulled my hat over my eyes because I was starting to tear up, and I told my therapist Melissa that I needed a minute to myself. I began to cry and asked Melissa to turn off the TV, which was broadcasting none other than Opening Day. Nothing like kicking me in the groin just a bit harder.

As if sent from the heavens, I see this beautiful young blond girl come walking in with a noticeable limp. She hopped up on her training table, pulled off her sweats that snapped up the sides, and popped her leg off. I never cried as hard as I did at that moment for someone who, at the time, I didn't even know. I felt excruciating agony at the thought that a young girl who has yet to experience so much in life could remain so upbeat despite the life-changing blow she had been dealt.

I have been figuratively slapped firmly in the face countless times since my incident, solely to help me realize how lucky and blessed I am. I had no room to complain, because even though Opening Day would pass without me, my life would go on. I was reminded that this was simply a pebble in my spikes compared to what Bree and others have to endure. The strength that Breanna McMahon exhibits every day of her life fills me with a strength I had never before felt, and every time I doubt myself, I envision Bree and know that I, too, can persevere. It was at that moment that I committed to turning things around, and instead of Bree being there for me, I had to be there for her, because she was contending with a hell of a lot more than I was.

It is during such periods of reflection that I am able to re-examine how I have done things and will try to do things differently from here on out. This is my refresher course to get on a path where I am never quite sure where I will be taken. I now had a full year to make some important decisions about my future and to determine what I could do to ensure that I was prepared to put in the necessary commitment to reestablish myself as a top-quality, major-league pitcher.

Another few days of recovery fell from the calendar, and Easter Sunday—the day of renewal and resurrection—arrived. I had an amazing day as my wife made our Easter a memorable event. I refused to look back at the fact that our original plans were to celebrate the holiday in Chicago, had I been pitching for the Indians. I just hoped that all I put into making it back to the show would pay off and I could drive on a smoothly paved road for the first time in my career. I have been shaped and molded through all the misfortune and injuries. They say that through trying times, you experience growth. I already have grown rhino skin, as all that's come my way has hardened me.

I was soon almost three weeks into rehabbing my knee, and I really had nothing new to report. Opening Day came and went, and the Indians lost to the White Sox 6-0. Short of hitting a pinch-hit grand slam and a three-run homer to boot, I can't imagine that I could have added anything to bring them a victory. I got my daily dose of Bree at rehab and bawled my eyes out, because I wished I could be as spirited as she was. I had so much love and respect for this girl—a girl I didn't even know. I also received news the Indians were checking to see if I really needed to rehab every day of the week. What the hell was that all about? They questioned Melissa to see if that was what I needed to be doing. This is the side of the game that doesn't fly with me. I had major surgery in which they selected my doctor, and then they questioned my protocol regarding what needed to be done to return me to pro-athlete form. It seemed rather contradictory that they would elect to send me to one of the world's premier surgeons and then break my balls when it came to how many days of rehab were prescribed.

Baseball had turned its back on me, but the funny thing was that I had never felt more confident. I had been in that position before. We ended the day by visiting our friends around the corner at their home decor store. There, hanging on the wall, was a real rhino head. Talk about ironic! I often alluded to the rhino skin I'd grown in order to wade through all this crap without losing my freaking mind.

Later in the week, I achieved my goal range-of-motion of 48 degrees. My leg was moving more smoothly, but not without some stiffness and pain. I am so in tune with my body as an athlete that I knew I would be able to tell if I was overdoing it and perhaps needed to back off, but at least for that day, I was determined to push myself a bit harder. It wasn't just about learning to walk without a limp, as a non-athlete would be encouraged to strive for. It was about my livelihood; if I got lazy and didn't push myself to the limit, I would never recover to the level I needed to continue my career. Envision a concert pianist who is trying to overcome arthritis, or a tightrope walker trying to overcome vertigo. It's not just about feeling better; it's about vocational survival.

All I could think of were my new inspirations: Bree McMahon and Nate Winters. Two people who, at such a young age, had to deal with a difficult hand of cards. I stopped feeling sorry for myself the minute I saw how bad those two amazing heroes had it. For those who don't know their heart-wrenching tales, allow my saga to sit on the bench for a few minutes while their stories take the hill.

Bree was a senior at Freedom High School in Orlando, Florida, in September of 2009. According to Bree's coaches, there was no doubt Bree was going to go on to play college soccer the following season. The only question was how high of a level she would reach.

Bree lived, breathed, and slept the sport, and even before her accident, she was an inspiration to her teammates through her enthusiasm and commitment to soccer.

On a warm Saturday morning in September, Bree and her teammates from the Freedom High Patriots girls' soccer team held a car wash as a fundraiser to help offset costs of a tournament in Raleigh, North Carolina. Bree's role that morning alternated between collecting donations from would-be patrons who drove by and lathering up the cars.

As Bree manned the hose and waited for the next car to pull in, her friend and teammate Chelsea Lingelbach hopped behind the wheel of an SUV to pull it in for a wash. Chelsea's foot was wet from the activity of the day, and her sneaker slipped off the brake and hit the accelerator, pinning her teammate between the vehicle and the wall.

Bree suffered major crushing injuries to both of her legs, and despite a valiant effort to save them both, her left leg had to be amputated within the first few days of her injury. Her right leg had to undergo major surgery and has had several muscles removed. She also spent six days in a drug-induced coma because of the injury. So as you can see, my little boo-boo wasn't anything when compared to what Bree has had to endure and overcome.

Nate Winter's story hits even closer to home for me, because Nate was a promising young pitcher for Winter Park High School before suffering a devastating and life-changing injury in August of 2008. Nate had a good fastball that peaked in the low 80s as a high school junior and, like me, he lived each day to play baseball.

One summer afternoon, Nate, his brother Zach, and a few of their buddies took the Winters' boat out for an afternoon spin on Lake Maitland, outside of Orlando. After one lap around the island, Nate was inexplicably tossed from the passenger seat into the water before being run over by the boat.

The propeller under the boat hit Nate's back in three places, including his ribs, and came just inches from puncturing his lung. It cut directly through his right Achilles and his right foot in multiple places and sliced through his left leg above the knee, cutting his femoral artery.

An article I read in *Orlando Magazine* after meeting Nate for the first time explains the extent of Nate's injuries after the seventeen-year-old was fished from the water by his brother and friends. "From mid-thigh to mid-calf, Nate's left leg had gone through a blender. His left foot was unscathed, but it was barely attached by a mishmash of muscle and skin. His entire right side looked as if he'd been hacked with a machete. His right foot was split lengthwise down the middle, his Achilles was severed, and he had gashes on his thigh, buttocks, waist, and rib cage."

So once again, after learning of the trials of my two inspirations, Bree and Nate, I was no longer the most unfortunate athlete in the room.

The weekend arrived, although when you are a recovering ballplayer, there really isn't a hell of a lot of difference between a weekend and a weekday. I couldn't remember the last time I'd had a full weekend off during the season. It was a weird feeling plugging into normal life without baseball. I believe that baseball is what I do, it isn't who I am, but when it is taken from you, you realize that may not be entirely true. Baseball is a bigger part of me than I realized and has brought me a collision of pleasure and pain.

As the weekend passed, I immediately learned that a full weekend off from physical therapy is not a good thing once Monday morning rolls around. Upon my arrival at PT, I had to sit on the ottoman and bend the leg not quite to standard on the goniometer, which is a protractor-like object used to measure the number of degrees a joint is able to bend. Funny that everything is measured in metrics, which is a French creation, but for some reason it was named after the Greeks. These are the things I thought of when I would normally be contemplating how to strike out guys.

Another 10 degrees of mobility was the highlight of my Wednesday. Not quite as exciting as hearing the sounds of the organ or the day's hot pop hits blaring over the PA during batting practice, while fans screamed for a ball like their lives depended on it. As the saying goes, "You don't know what you got until it's gone." It was April 15th, and I missed my sport more than I ever could have imagined. I have baseball engrained in my head: my favorite green grass at Kauffman Stadium, the laughter that fills the bus ride to and from hotels and airports, the smell of my glove, and the electricity in the park before the first pitch is even thrown. My motivation to return to all of that was embedded in my every fiber, because it was taken away so quickly merely by planting my foot and then watching and hearing my knee fold like an empty water bottle.

In a strange way, I had comfort in knowing there was a reason behind it. I would emerge as if I were a new draft pick. I knew people would talk about me and say that I was washed up, stunk, no longer had it, and was prone to injury, instead of realizing that I had taken the road less traveled to get back to the Big Leagues each and every time. It is hard to get to the show at all, and it is even harder to stay there, but I was not going to let that setback turn me into a has-been.

I received my direct deposit from the Indians and saw that the deposit was about $20,000 less than what I was used to receiving. Instead of getting down in the dumps, I got a bit more motivated. It's not easy living a rather lavish lifestyle, then getting a nasty taste of reality. This is the state of the economy we are in today. Many people are feeling the heat of the financial strain, and although I realize that a ballplayer makes substantially more than the average

American, it's all relative.

I didn't let this reality check detract from the highlights of my day, however. I overcame my restriction of 55 degrees mobility from the day prior and set my sites on 60 degrees. Seeing my family, spending some time shooting Nerf hoops, and wrestling with my son wasn't the same as pitching against Texas (the team we would have been playing), but it wasn't half bad. I'm not saying I could get used to it, but there was a bright side to having that unexpected time to get to know my son and reconnect with Danielle.

I even received some encouragement from former teammate Sean Casey, who is unequivocally one of the best men in the game of baseball. Casey, a dear friend, said stepping away from the grind of the game could be a blessing. He may have been right if I had a bank account and wasn't relying on baseball as my bread and butter, but I understood what he meant, and I was starting to think that he could be right on so many levels.

This reminded me of how I felt when I played the role of Curious George at my son's first birthday party. I rented the costume and sauntered into the backyard dressed up as the world's most famous monkey. Many of my own relatives did not know it was me, and it was fun messing with people who hadn't realized that I had disappeared from the crowd. You would think that the birthday boy's 6'5" father being missing and the monkey being 6'5" would be a dead giveaway, but I guess not. Through the eyes of the mask, I looked out and saw how the kids adored George. The parents seemed equally thrilled.

Fortunately, time was plentiful. I am glad that I kept my mind positive. It wasn't a front, but was how I truly felt. I was so locked in and couldn't wait for the next sunrise to see if I'd gotten my knee to bend a bit further than the day before. So many times, we go through our days without tangible goals. By having to measure my success by increase in movement, it kept me focused and driven with a measurable goal to determine victory versus failure each day. The day I reached 60 degrees, like Balboa, I screamed, "Yo, Adrian. I did it!"

CHAPTER 9

To Cheat or Not to Cheat

> *"The first and worst of all frauds is to cheat one's self. All sin is easy after that."*
> *~ Pearl Bailey*

My hero was human after all. Up to that point, my girl Bree had been solid as a rock. She had ice water in her veins, like an MLB closer has to have, and I'd never seen her leave therapy without a save or a "W" in the win column. She had been there for me on days that I wobbled, and I never saw this girl crack. I thought I understood her pain, but actually only saw a glimpse into her world. I was thoroughly impressed how a young girl could handle such a drastic change in her life. This day was different, though. It seemed for the first time, my heroine needed me. I tried to pick her up and make her laugh, but once again, God's timing is perfect. In walked a woman who was mentally challenged, or perhaps senile. She went off as she entered, causing a major disruption in the office. Even Bree's day, along with her attitude, was altered after seeing how things could be worse. It's all in your perspective.

"Tell Me Why I Don't Like Mondays" was the song playing on repeat that day. Who does, I guess, but mine seemed to be especially rancid those days, because I got stiff over the weekend from not bending the knee and not having rehab. I tried to do a bit on my own, but it wasn't the same as having the masters working their magic on this bird's wounded limb. This was a mentally tough day as well; the pain was manageable, but the rehab session took a lot out of me. Once again, Bree was there to inspire me. The pebble in my shoe was nothing like what she contended with. I would take the pain all day long so I would not slow down, because she didn't. I was frustrated over crutches, while she had to put on a whole new leg. It's all relative. I could get emotional over what I was going through, but my situation was temporary, not a permanent, life-altering event like this gal had to adjust to.

The mental preparation of baseball doesn't take place only before a game. It is an ongoing and never-ending process. It is like having that yellow man talking to you in your head as Seal describes in his song "Crazy." I believe it is a bit like going crazy. That's why you often see players with routines or tics. They are afraid to stray from doing something that worked once for them and, in essence, become a victim of their own neurotic habits. Tell me how it worked out for Milton and his red stapler in the movie *Office Space*. Sure, he got the last laugh, but in the real world, his psychosis wasn't acceptable, and he was banished to the basement. In extreme events like baseball, the neurosis is part of the art form.

As I thought about my recovery, I knew it wasn't a slam dunk (if I may borrow a phrase from a rival sport) that I'd make it all the way back. The worst-case scenario was that I'd never get to play again. I wasn't going to let that happen, but I knew the possibility existed. I believe it's important not to confuse effort and results. Michael

Jordan's inability to make his high school basketball team is well-documented, but we don't find the names of his high school teammates Allan Baldwin, Thomas Riley, Michael Brag, Larry Jordan, Leroy Smith, or Joe LaBoo in the annals of NBA history, do we?

It was also possible that having temporary downtime to recover and heal could allow me to continue playing baseball even longer. Doubts crept into my head because the future was not promised. When we worry about the two scariest days of our lives—yesterday and tomorrow—we never come to terms with the fact that the only day we can control is today. Live for the gift that is now. That is why they call it *the present.*

Of course, the best-case scenario was that I could make it back 110 percent. This could happen with a lot of hard work and determination. I marked it on the calendar. I couldn't change the fact that, by the time I was healed, the season would be completely over. I marked down my target date as the beginning of spring training 2011, and I was taking each day one at a time.

In flight on my way to a check-up in Vail, I thought of how well the therapy was going, albeit conservative. I couldn't do much to change that, though, and I was praying that I could ditch my crutches after the visit and start some normal activity. I would never take my health for granted again. I can totally sympathize with those who have a handicap, no matter if it's permanent or temporary. I had been a bit bitter inside, because I tended to compare myself to others, and this wasn't fair.

I have always tried to do the right thing and rationalize why people say good things happen to good people, knowing that sometimes it seems to go the other way. There will always be "what ifs" in life. There will always be a question of whether or not I did the right thing. I had been programmed to have baseball in my life for so long that I didn't know what I would do without it. There were a couple of reasons I couldn't walk away yet. The money was too great, and my livelihood was in jeopardy. Moreover, my prideful heart couldn't accept that unhappy ending.

God knew I didn't love the game like I should have at this point in my career. I had become a little bitter because of the behind-the-scenes shit that constantly messes with your head. People only see what happens between the lines on game day during the three hours and fifteen minutes we are on the stage. Unfortunately, the business side is what they aren't privy to: the labels, the favoritism, the economics, and the people who have never played baseball making decisions about our livelihood. Not having complete control of your career unless you are a "made" guy is a pretty helpless feeling.

I was supposed to have been somewhat of that type, one of the golden boys, but I never got through the stage where I earned the experience needed to become a "made" guy. Oftentimes in this game, your name is put up on a magnet board or scribbled on cocktail napkin by people sitting in meeting rooms who decide your fate. "Does he have any options or outrights left to control his rights?" Winning in the minor leagues has merit to fans. The organization is constantly developing and building, so if a an organization isn't winning at the Big League level, some minor league teams will stock up on Big League talent in order to win at AAA and load up with insurance policies.

At the time of my injury, I was tired of moving my family around and being told I had a mechanical flaw or what my pregame routine should be. Regardless of how strong you are mentally, that shit messes with your head. I didn't make excuses. I could admit when I sucked or got lucky in a game. I also knew there were variables that would continue to work against me, and I tried to put myself in a position to be so strong and so dominant they couldn't help but overlook their preconceived notion of who I was. I put on my blinders so I couldn't pay attention to the business side of baseball as the game itself played. I went about my business as if it were not that important.

I became really good at evaluating how people operated. At the tail end of my stay in Texas, I told my agent I wouldn't be there next year. I had a gut feeling, because at the end of the year, I could hardly pitch after coming back from a bout with forearm tendonitis. Once again, I just kept asking myself if that was what I wanted, and if it was worth all my efforts. *Dear Lord, I sure hope so. You have given me the gift of perseverance. Let me use it to show my resilience. Amen.*

I also prayed that my alternate god, Dr. Steadman, would give me some good news. I prayed it would be better than the news he gave me when I first met him. That with hard work and determination, there was no reason I couldn't come back stronger than ever. *God, if You are listening, please let there be a story of success at the end of all this. I know I am sharing my plans with You, but I hope they align with Yours. I hope and pray to be able to play winter ball next year.*

For some reason, it was easy to have down days, no matter how hard I tried to stay positive. I had been able to draw on my strength and positive mindset, calling on the Lord's strength while mixing in some reading of inspirational books filled with positive affirmations during my downtime. It's sort of the "fake it till you make it" principle. Immerse yourself in a pool of positive thoughts, and some of them are bound to wash off on you.

I had been going strong to that point, but that week I hit a bit of a wall. Mentally, I was exhausted, and I realized that it had not been easy on my family or me. I continued to have concerns about the future, and wondering what came next constantly played on my mind. I loved and respected the game so much, but the reality was that I may never play again.

I asked myself what I guess are understandable thoughts. *Should I sell my soul to the devil and cheat myself and the game? Should I do whatever it takes to get back like so many other guys have done?* I envisioned the little devil dude perched on my right shoulder saying, "Do it, Cheese," while prodding me in the side of the neck with his pointed pitchfork. "Do it, Cheese." Many have benefitted by making that deal with the devil.

Performance enhancers have been used by many players to get back to that point, but not me. I am actually pissed that I allowed the thought to cross my mind. For so much of my career, I was naive to the fact that so many guys were using these drugs. I refused to believe it during the early parts of my career, but I realized that if the integrity of the game hadn't been so important to me, I, too, would have used them to my advantage. Tears began streaming down my face.

There were many reasons for my tears. This game and business can be so harsh on the body and on the inner self. I'd also been thinking of my pal and inspiration, Bree, a lot lately. It's funny how athletes understand each other. There is a bond there, no matter the sport or the age. The conviction and fraternity-like attitude brings you close to one another because you understand the drive, the concerns, and the insurmountable challenges that each other face.

I cried that day for me, but more so for her. I was so mad that things like that happened to someone so deserving of a better fate. To add to my own emotional pain, Danielle's uncle died of a sudden heart attack that day at age fifty-one. More emotional and physical tears flooded my tear ducts. As I battled those demons, my therapist busily cranked my leg toward 70 degrees. I screamed at the top of my lungs, as I felt like I was getting close to the point where only a few degrees difference made it feel like she was trying to bend a popsicle stick.

Bree walked in for a therapy session and informed me that she had to have her fourteenth surgery to clean out an infection. How could I ever even think about complaining over the hand I'd been dealt? I hurt so badly for this young lady that I hardly even knew what to say. I only had a slight morsel of understanding of what she was going through, and yet I had total compassion for her circumstances. The girl wanted nothing more than to dance at her prom, and now she might have to attend in a wheelchair. I witnessed a glimpse of how bad things can be for others, and therefore I was so grateful for all I had.

Each day, either Danielle or my good friend, Tim Bratcher, would drop me off at the same spot, and my short walk to the PT office reminded me of that walk to the clubhouse. I pretended it was a walk to the clubhouse, since I would be taking this walk for a while. That week had been tough, and I was trying to draw on every ounce of positive mental attitude I could muster inside. It was the same feeling I had when I came in with bases loaded and no outs in relief. Mentally, I was prepared to battle some tough days, but even my elbow wasn't this tough. Up to that point, the pain I encountered during Tommy John surgery was the litmus by which I gauged my pain tolerance. This pain, however, could not even be measured on the same scale. It soared right off the charts.

I actually had a few fans show up while I was getting my treatment, and it made me feel like a ballplayer instead of an invalid. There are a ton of young gymnasts who came in for PT. They were so bubbly and enthusiastic that their exuberance helped me get through each painstaking session toward the next degree of mobility.

My quote of the day was "Champions don't reach for the stars. They climb a mountain and grab one." I did that, and I grabbed one. Little did I know that I also grabbed a pink heart, a yellow moon, two green clovers, a blue diamond, and a purple horse shoe. Thank my Lucky Charms that I grabbed that horseshoe, because I needed all the luck I could get.

We bent to 66 degrees, not without a share of pain and anguish, but successfully, nonetheless. I only hoped the loud moaning and excruciating groans they may have heard did not scare the people who called to schedule an appointment that day. That was not someone giving birth behind closed doors; it was me trying to gain one more degree—one more degree closer to standing on that mound again.

I tried to gain perspective on all that was laid out in front of me. I went to Nate's ballgame and witnessed this kid—who had a 1 in 10,000 chance of even living—take the mound and pitch again. Talk about perspective.

At one point in my life, I was awestruck at the thought of meeting Nolan Ryan, and then I finally got to meet him in Texas. Now I was equally awestruck by meeting a group of kids who congregated at a high school game in support of Nate and his inspirational comeback story. Meeting him was personal for me. It taught me volumes about self-esteem and confidence. God clearly put Nate in my path to prevent me from wallowing in misery. I was so sympathetic toward those amazing individuals who I had the honor to meet. Though I hadn't so much as taken a step in their shoes, I totally appreciated some of what they were going through: having to adapt to life-changing events and overcome the roadblocks that God placed in our paths.

I hated my crutches and was so frustrated that it had been two months since I practically had them surgically implanted into my armpits. I honestly didn't know how I would cope with another surgery, let alone losing a limb. Baseball is such a huge part of me that maybe God felt the need to unravel the selfish desires of my heart and remind me what is really important.

There is a Higher Power at work, constantly molding us to conform to His perception of the big picture. I am so grateful that I was able to take in a high school game that day and see an amazing young man whose love for the game drove him to not only get a new leg, but to return to the mound he loves and pitch in front of a crowd of nearly 500 people. The purity of the experience erased all that has been tainted by steroids and greed in the game today. I got a real refreshing dose of reality, and I loved every minute of it. Thank you, Nate, for showing me what real guts in life mean. You were an inspiration to me. Though Jayse was with me, he didn't realize what he witnessed that day because he was only two years old. I will remind him of your story forevermore.

CHAPTER 10

SITTING DOWN WITH THE HOME RUN KING

---///---

"It's not the name that makes the player. It's the player. If all sons of players could play in the major leagues, they'd all be up here, but they're not."

~ Barry Bonds

The end of April was upon us, and instead of thinking of my end-of-month-one pitching stats, as I normally would be, I was striving for 80 degrees of movement. I made that familiar trip from Florida to Vail to check in with Steadman. After arriving and waiting for over two hours to see him, I got great news that all looked great, and my recovery was right on schedule. I talked with him for only about two minutes, but the good news was worth the wait. All I had was time, and yet it felt like I didn't have any time at all. It seemed as if I was busier than I had ever been, getting reacquainted with my family and watching my son grow without being whisked away on road trips in between visits home. I didn't wish away time, because every moment was a blessing, but as my crutches dug into my armpits, they were a constant reminder that I was not where I needed to be.

I started on some exercises I watched others perform the day after my surgery. I was so anxious to get to that point. April 27th was my turn to start. I was at 71 degrees by myself and was able to reach 74 degrees on my first PT session of the day. The exercise bike was a thrill to ride, despite the agitation that made my knee joint feel as if, at any moment, it might duplicate the first horrible experience. I trusted Steadman's workmanship, and I knew that I would structurally push myself to the max.

In between sessions, I spent some time enjoying the only nice day in Vail—until the winds started rolling in. I sat on the patio of the Sonnenalp Resort and tried to record a video for my company, Perfect Pitch Marketing. The wind blew so strongly that it swiped the microphone from my hand and blew an umbrella across the patio that landed against the side of my head. This 75-pound patio umbrella hit me so hard, I saw stars. Funny thing was, I recorded the whole episode and can likely win $25,000 on *America's Funniest Home Videos*, if I decide to send it in. That's one way to supplement my income. Needless to say, after that take, it was a wrap. It was easy to laugh at myself after living through the knee experience, and Lord knows I needed all the laughs I could get. I even shared the video of that day at PT session number two, and some of the therapists were appreciative that I was able to laugh at myself, despite having a knot on the side of my head the size of Sanibel Island.

Despite being the end of April in Vail, winter rolled in the next morning and I froze along with the disgruntled locals who anxiously waited for summer to begin. I reached 77 degrees flexibility, and Dr. Steadman gave me another Steadman Stamp of Approval that things were progressing well. I counted on the next two weeks to rid myself of crutches and have the freedom to drive.

A month had passed, and my thoughts hadn't wavered much, although it was harder to watch baseball continue on without me. I wouldn't even turn the TV to any station that I knew would be showing games, as I couldn't deal with the agony of the show going on without me. There was no indifference within me; it was just a phase of getting through it. I hate to say it, but I became a pro at dealing with adversity. There was no glory in it. There sure wasn't a multi-year contract waiting for me to sign any time soon. I tried to keep my PT sessions light. My PT group laughed, and I tried to set a tone in the office because I made so much grunting noise when I tried to get past my threshold of pain. I'd get pissed when I rode the bike, knowing that I'd have to endure the heartache and physical pain to make it back. I looked up at the window of the PT office where there were silhouettes of sports figures, the one right in front of me being a swinging batter. It sparked anger as I pushed the pedal harder to increase my range of motion. Five days a week, I had to endure that crap with no glory and no one cheering. There remained an audience of one, and I knew He watched over me while I rode. I remembered that my pal Bree was in and out of the hospital, dealing with surgery after surgery, and I once again gained perspective.

I hated that my family was also being dragged through the experience. My wife and son sat in the car nearly all day, because I couldn't drive. My appointments were scheduled at the times when my son napped, so he'd sleep in the car while my wife studied for her real estate exam. She wanted to have a hand in our future. With the gift I had been granted and the work I'd put in to achieve great things in this incredible game, there was no way my wife should have to work to ensure our family's ultimate survival. I knew it could be worse. I wasn't dealing with a terminal disease or something life threatening, but when you can't play baseball after dedicating your whole life to the game you love, it sure feels terminal, especially

My first Big League jersey.

The nickname "GrillCheese" has stood the test of time.

Wanted to be with Dad as much as possible, especially at the ballpark.

My love for the game and inner drive
started at an early age.

A special memory with Dad and Vada Pinson.

Growing up in dugouts and clubhouses helped me become an outlier of baseball.

Even on Halloween, all I wanted to be was a Big Leaguer just like Dad.

Championships were won when Baldwinsville and Liverpool talent played together in Central New York.

Radisson Little League - Following Dad's footsteps started way back when.

Dad as our pitching coach for Seneca River North Little League.

Taking in a Blue Jays game, a frequent visit and drive from Syracuse.

Nick and Catherine Giampietro were always there.

Building my "field of dreams" in my backyard.

14/15-year-old Liverpool Pool & Spa Central NY State Champs.

Gaining attention from local scouts selected by the Yankees in 1994.

Syracuse send off to play for Team Italy in 1996 Olympics.

Baldwinsville Bees, 1994 High School Section III Champs.

Father knows best.

4th overall pick in the 1997 draft.

Draft day at home - Celebrating with my closest friends and family.

Alan Marr joined me at my draft party at home in Baldwinsville.

Syracuse local media capturing the beginning of my Road to the Show.

In San Fransisco at Candlestick to get signing bonus and meet the team.

Signed my contract with San Fransisco at the Ocean Edge with Alan Marr.

Celebrating a dream come true with a great family but missing a great friend - Tim Metzger (TM), you will always inspire me.

Name on the back allows you to play for the one on the front.

Got to hang with my sister after a Big East Conference game weekend at Seton Hall University.

Participated in the first Futures All Star Game in 1999.

2006 ALCS Championship Season Ring Ceremony at Comerica Park.

Ring ceremony in 2006 ALCS.

Celebrating with Sean Casey and the Detroit faithful in 2006.

Family day in Denver with Danielle, Mom, Steph, Jayse, and nephew Drew.

Hoping for a third generation Grilli in the Show.

2009 World Baseball Classic in Skydome.

Spring training 2011: Defying the odds after surgery and rocking #93 in the Phillies bullpen (at least they put my name on the back of my jersey).

Red Carpet Ride in NYC 2013 All-Star Gala with Danielle and Jayse.

© Mark Cunningham

Career dream highlight sharing my first All-Star Game with my boys during HR derby.

Mariano Rivera, the greatest reliever of all time!

Taking time to let it all sink in...

© Mark Cunningham

Five Pittsburgh Pirates representing during lineup.

Kodak moment with dominating relief pitchers Mark Melancon, Craig Kimbrel, and Aroldis Chapman.

Firing in the 9th at Citi Field in 2013 ASG.

Randy Hadley (good friend and personal trainer), Amie Russell, Melissa Brown (physical therapist), and Breanna McMahon (my inspiration and friend in physical therapy).

After 20 years, the city of Pittsburgh finally got their winning season.

Celebrating spring training with good friend, Breanna McMahon.

Breanna making the dream her reality!

Whipping! On stage with Pearl Jam kicking off Lightning Bolt tour in Pittsburgh.

when you're thirty-three years old.

I had a sudden flashback to my first spring training with the Giants, and I recalled standing in the outfield with some new draft picks. They were in mid-discussion about who was the first pick for the team. I played along since they didn't know I was that pick. They marveled they hadn't heard any stories about the team's new guy. They were talking about last year's pick from 1996 and mocked the guy because he just sat in the outfield and ate apples during BP. It was the norm to test the waters as a first rounder if you weren't taught to love and respect the game. I was old-school because my dad played. I felt like I had a distinct advantage, since I had a father who played during an era when things were much different. So I listened and played along for a while, until I could no longer keep it in. I finally said, "Hello, fellas. It is me, Jason Grilli, your ninety-seven first-round draft pick. Want to get some lunch after our day is out?" They were taken aback and extremely apologetic to my face. They fumbled over their words a bit and said I didn't act like a first-round pick. I knew the drill coming in—there would be a lot of animosity for getting the money I got. I didn't approach it that way, and I told some of the coaches out of the gate that I didn't want any preferential treatment. The fiftieth pick and I put on our pants the same way, and I wanted to do as much, if not more, to prove to the guys that I was serious about becoming a better ballplayer.

The only other incident during that spring-training season reminded me of *Top Gun*. We were about to play competitive games, and we had to scrimmage the Big League team. They told me during team stretch that I was on the hill that day, and who did I get to face but Barry Bonds, who was batting third. All the guys were yelling, "He's going to hit a 600-foot bomb off you, Grilli. I bet you dinner tonight he takes you deep." Well, I turned toward my less-than-supportive teammates and said, "I'll tell you what. If he does, I will take all you guys out for a steak dinner tonight, but if I strike him out, you guys take me out." The bet was on.

I played out in my mind what that experience would be like. I didn't care about facing Bill Mueller or Darryl Hamilton at the top of the order as much as I cared about facing Bonds. My thoughts brought me back to Little League. You simulate in your mind that you are facing the best hitters in the major leagues the entire time you're growing up. "Now stepping into the box against eleven-year-old fire-baller Jason Grilli is Barry Bonds."

Well, I was grown up now, and as I looked at Bonds stepping into the box, I pinched myself, as this was the most real situation of my career. *This isn't Little League, Cheese. It is real.*

All the guys from the front office and my buddy Dan McKinley's mom sat behind home plate. My adrenaline was pumping, yet I was reasonably calm, knowing I had everything to gain and nothing to lose…except maybe some pride and the baseball I was holding. I pumped a few sinkers in there that Bonds fouled straight back. I had enough on it to get ahead 0-2. I then threw him two great curveballs on which the umpire refused to call him out. After all, this was a scrimmage. With the count now 2-2, I pumped another fastball up and inside that was taken for ball three. I threw two more sinkers that he fought off foul.

He had pride on the line going into this, and we all know Bonds has an ego to uphold. I thought that if I was going to strike this sucker out, I had to make him swing. There would be no strike three called today, son, first pick or not. This was Barry Mother-Bleeping Bonds in the box, and I needed to find a way to get him out. Well, a change-up was in my mind. My catcher threw down the signs, and I shook several times to get my pitch. Best bullet with a lot riding on that pitch already. I pulled the string, and just like it was in slo-mo, Bonds swung and took a mighty whiff. Strike three.

Bonds muttered loud enough for me to hear, "Who organized this minor league shit?" as he flipped his bat in the air. I couldn't wait to call home. High fives were all over the dugout, and apparently there were some in the stands as well. Mrs. McKinley was there with the front office, and she said they were even exchanging fives. I guess there was no love lost for Barry, since his ego was something people tiptoed around. After all, he is—or was—a supposed Hall of Famer, and they knew what they were expecting to get out of him during the season. As for me, maybe I earned a stripe that day among my peers and the front office that justified them signing me. Boy, oh boy, did everything seem promising then.

Mother's Day arrived and the following day, Danielle, Jayse, and I went to see the movie *How to Train Your Dragon*. At the end of the movie, the main character, Hiccup, ends up with a prosthetic leg. If God wasn't speaking to me then, I don't know when He was. I don't think anything could be more vivid than that experience. I turned to Danielle and said there was something bigger going on behind that movie scene. There had to be. There was something big behind it all. A message, a lesson, maybe something else. I wasn't sure what it was, but I trusted in it.

Another ten-day stretch passed, and we were on the north side of 90 degrees, which they said would be the hardest part of therapy. If I could not get beyond 90 degrees, there was a possibility of having to go back for a scope. I was fighting hard to avoid going that route. My best defense against all of it was humor, and if I had to be in therapy for over three hours, then I was going to try to have a good time. I'd seen all the patients that walked through the door, and I'd developed relationships with them. Like at Vail, misery loves company, but we tried to leave out the misery part and just enjoy each other's company. We fought the battle together, climbing to the top of our own respective mountains. Most were not athletes and I was the only pro, but we each had a road to travel and a goal to achieve. We each refused to give in to the innate desire to take it easy on ourselves, and whenever anyone in the room looked like he was about to fall, someone on our team was there to pick him up.

It was a great day all around, and I was enjoying therapy a lot more since I was seeing my hard work pay off. I was also enjoying my last few months before Bree headed to college in the fall. I witnessed a great award ceremony when she and Nate were honored for high school varsity sports. The *Orlando Sentinel* put on the event, and I became emotional once again. Knowing the two and seeing them heal and reach the next level made me feel like I was part of something I was meant to experience.

June 8th passed, and I achieved 120 degrees. I was pretty damn happy with myself, and I was ready for my next check-up in Vail with Steadman. I thought they'd be pleasantly surprised with my progress. The uneasiness of not making my mark on baseball and earning about 10 percent of what I was accustomed to earning made me realize how lucky and special it is to have a chance to play baseball and put on that uniform. Every time I hit therapy, I pushed a little bit harder, and the zest to get to the next level kept me going.

I headed into week seventeen of recovery, and I had attained full range of motion ahead of the planned schedule. I accomplished what I set out to do for phase one of my process, and I now needed to get my strength back quickly so I could begin to throw in August. I still had hopes to play winter ball, before going to spring training in February. You begin to doubt if that will happen when your leg gives out as you try to walk fast. I didn't wonder about how I would deliver a pitch as much as if I could cover first base like I used to. Those were the thoughts I had to contend with on a daily basis.

Sitting with my son, I dreamt that I would be able to share what I have been through. I pulled out my scrapbook and placed it on the floor to look at what I had compiled before Jayse was born. I knew I would not have time to organize it all while on a fast pace, but now I was sitting there flipping the pages with Jayse as he shouted out, "Baseball!" As much as I treasured that moment sitting with my little guy, I had to get back, and I was driven to do that. I was trapped in the midst of monotony. I saw a battle where my desire was strong, and I prayed my body responded as quickly as I needed it to.

The night was also special since an old friend and dear teammate, Mike Hessman from the Toledo/Detroit days, drove up to visit us. It is always interesting to see how guys stick it out in this game and how it can trap you. Hessman was drafted in 1996 by the Atlanta Braves, and it took him seven years before he made his major league debut. His first MLB hit was a home run four days after his call-up. Today he is the active minor league home run leader with just under 400, including almost 275 at the AAA level.

He was working so hard, having his best season, and hoped to go play in Japan, but as luck would have it, he got hit with a pitch and fractured his hand. He was now in Port St. Lucie rehabbing, so he stopped over to enjoy a barbecued steak. It was great to catch up and laugh over some good memories. It was amazing that four or five years had passed since we'd won the Governor's Cup in Toledo. That was the cherry on top for me that season, after being told they needed me to pitch in AAA.

The Tigers struggled, and the team was not going anywhere. I was not on the roster that spring. As it goes in baseball, if you don't have money and are not on the forty-man roster, all you can do is hope and pray for the best. I was the last cut that spring and was sent to Toledo. After they sent me down, I approached Alan Trammell and Tiger GM Dave Dombrowski and expressed my dissatisfaction with the way the demotion was handled, because I was sick and tired of the same bullshit reasons that no coach likes to admit to when they send you down. I told them when it was time to win to find me and all the other good players that they optioned to AAA. We were so motivated to prove them wrong that we went out and won the Governor's Cup Championship in 2005. I felt slightly vindicated when they called me back up at the end of the season following our Governor's Cup success.

Making a living out of this game is really hard, harder than bending your knee after surgery. It makes you wonder how some people stick in AAA for so long and are trapped in the game. I felt for Hessman. He, like so many others who have gone that route, was just trying to make a living and provide for his family. The game becomes humbling when you are out of it. I just prayed I could continue to fight and have the courage to show what I was made of. What was important that evening was sharing time with a friend who was going through his own struggles and obstacles, perhaps even far greater than mine were.

CHAPTER 11

BUILDING A BROTHERLY BOND

> *"There is no better (lesson) than adversity. Every defeat, every heartbreak, every loss, contains its own seed, its own lesson on how to improve your performance the next time."*
>
> ~ Malcolm X

Envision a slender, twenty-two-year-old kid still trying to fill out his 6'5" frame at 190 pounds. He sheepishly walks into a downtown gym that is echoing to the rafters with the sounds of club music and bursting to the rafters with dudes who have necks that begin at their ears and travel down to what used to be their shoulders. Well, that was the scene in the year 2000 after I'd just had my first surgery, and I was the 190-pound kid.

My elbow had a stress fracture that scared the death out of me with a big screw to hold it together, thanks to the handiwork of Dr. Andrews. My motivation to get well was brought about because I had surgery early enough; I had time to come back from this setback. At least that was my driving force and my impetus to hit the weight room. As I stated earlier, one coach at Marlin Fest had made it clear that he didn't think it was possible for me to do that. Well, shame on you, Coach. It's amazing what happens when you pour gasoline on a fire that is already pretty darn hot.

There I was, a skinny, string bean of a kid who knew nothing about weight training, and for the first time in my career, I was admittedly tempted with the notion of doing steroids, like so many of my baseball brethren. After two potential career-ending injuries, I was faced with a real life decision. Do I do it the easy way, like so many who currently litter the rosters of baseball? Or do I do it the Steve Grilli way and the Jason Grilli way—through hard work, blood, sweat, and toil? Though I clearly know right from wrong and have been brought up to have respect for the game I love, I would be lying if I said I wasn't tempted to take a shot in the ass and make my road back a whole lot easier. But I'm better than that, and I was not going to listen to that little red devil who resides on everyone's left shoulder on occasion. Easy is clearly not part of my make-up, and despite the fact that many are doing it, I'm not like those many.

Across the gym, I saw a 275-pound guy who looked like he could not only bench press a small automobile, but also like he'd spent a day or two working hard in the gym. He was lifting moderate weights and had a trusting, gentle look about him that made me want to ask for some advice. I used to live in the downtown area of Orlando where there was a small but popular gym owned by Ice, one of the American Gladiators. Ice was a woman with blond hair, and she was the biggest and strongest woman on the show. Up to that point, it was the closest I had ever been to someone who could crush me like a grape if I looked at him cross-eyed. Aside from the bulging biceps and the ripped abs, the two of them couldn't have looked more opposite.

I could tell that my pathetic workout was not all that impressive to him, because I kept catching him sizing me up as I did my best

Lou Ferrigno imitation. I knew he was also trying to figure out who I was, since I came in with all my baseball apparel on. I approached him and asked if he just worked out there, or if he did any personal training. He countered by asking if I played ball, and, of course, the conversation took on a life of its own from there. I explained who I was and where I was in my career and asked if we could work together. I was done trying to figure out this weight thing on my own. In fact, I was intimidated just by being there. I also made it very clear to him that I was fighting an internal battle of whether or not to join the ranks of the PED club that flooded MLB, and I also had infiltrated the gym rats who obviously didn't just eat a steady diet of egg whites and nutritional protein bars to get big and strong.

During my conversation with Randy Hadley, who would soon become my trainer, I continued explaining that I was a ballplayer coming off an injury, and I knew that I needed to compete with a talent pool that unfairly had an edge on me. I wanted to do this the right way, because my father taught me to love and respect this game. I even spoke to some other family members of mine who were in the pharmaceutical business, and they backed my decision to do my training the right way.

I explained to Randy that I needed a person who understood weights but I didn't need to find myself on the next cover of *Muscle Magazine*. I just needed to have functional strength for my position as a pitcher to keep up with myself. I can ignore all of the other nonsense I have seen in front of my face as long as I see the results I need through hard work, sweat, and proper training. After all, it will be far more gratifying to me to know I achieved it the same way my Italian brother Frank Sinatra suggested, "I did it my way." This is where my friendship with Randy Hadley officially began.

Randy became my Mr. Miyagi of sorts. He showed me technique before I could get into strength training. No, there wasn't the "Wax on" and "Wax off," and I certainly didn't paint Randy's fence, but Randy taught me many lessons about hard work and perseverance that I will carry with me forever.

We used very low weights and concentrated more on technique than on pumping insane amounts of weight. In my mind, I was saying, *Yes, this is hard, but when are we going to get stronger?* I needed to keep up with all the guys who were using junk to do less work in the offseason. He had me working girly-sized weights over and over again. Yet I knew in my heart that I had hired the master and needed to stick it out and hang with the lesson plan.

Randy reassured me not to worry, as we would never run out of weights in the weight room. I trusted him, since I was actually really sore after what appeared to be rather routine workouts. My daily routine at that particular time was to wake before the rooster did and open up HealthSouth, where I did rehab for my elbow for three hours beginning at 6:00 AM, finishing up around 9:00 AM. I then went home to grab some breakfast and take a quick nap before heading to the gym around eleven with Randy. I'd head out mid-afternoon to find a partner to play catch with, and then I would spend the evening hours working on some college courses before falling asleep on my keyboard.

Time was in short supply, and I had to squeeze in a full workday each and every day. By day's end, I'd exhausted myself physically and mentally. There was no other choice. Resting on my signing bonus was not going to help me eke out an existence. I knew what went into getting me to this point, and I was not taking it for granted.

Life was in limbo at that point, and I thought it couldn't get any more challenging. Just like when I was hitting rocks out in front of my house as a boy, I had another life-defining moment that would prepare me for something far greater—at least that was what I kept telling myself. It was extremely humbling to see baseball go on without me. It can knock you into the dumps if you allow it. The monotony that comes along with a boring schedule makes each day seem like it's twenty-five hours long, and every minute seems far longer than it does when everything is going the right way.

I saw progress that would have been unattainable had I not been lucky enough to find someone who was as passionate about what he was doing as I was. Randy wanted to find someone with whom to develop his reputation, and I wanted to find someone to nurse me back to health. Though a 275-pound, muscular man wasn't necessarily the nurse I had always envisioned, Randy would do just fine. It became a perfect marriage, because I needed him and he needed me. I was happy to help him, and from the beginning, mutual trust was solidly established and we worked extremely well together.

Randy and I became more than student and mentor, and in many ways, became more than a pair of friends. I think Randy and I became true brothers and shared not only physical growth together, but emotional and psychological development as well. There is not a man on the planet, short of my dad, who has grown to mean more to me than Randy.

We continued to work together for several off-seasons, and each time I spent time with Randy, I learned more and grew more confident. When I took off my street clothes and changed into my Superman costume, I could do so with confidence in the event that anyone taking shortcuts cared to notice. It was more important to me to keep up because I wanted to go through my career doing things the right way.

Each year, Randy and I begin our off-season workout regimen in early November. It is symbolic that the carving of the turkey and the subsequent food orgy that comes along with Thanksgiving Day has to be tempered, because I am knee-deep in off-season conditioning.

Just as sure as the Detroit Lions and the Dallas Cowboys were suiting up for their respective Turkey Day battles, I, too, was well underway in several intense weeks of training with Randy. Thus began the psychosis prior to the Thanksgiving festivities.

We start and end every season with a conversation to determine our goals and work on a regimen that will ensure success in attaining those goals. When you spend this much time with an individual, you build a relationship and bond moving forward. We spent four or five days a week for a couple hours each day over the next couple of months preparing for the season and striving toward a successful accomplishment of our goals. In doing that, not only did I get physically stronger, but my friendship with this incredible man also grew.

Randy saw me at some of my most vulnerable points when I'd ask the "whys" and "hows." He has been that pillar of strength to help get me through adversity. He has seen me come back from injury, fall in love and marry Danielle, and become a father with the births of Jayse and Jayden.

Randy helped me understand that everything in life has its purpose, whether they are good times or bad times, and you just have to work through them. Through our friendship, we created a certain kind of bond, because there are so many things behind the scenes that most people don't see. Randy became that confidant and that shoulder to me, and in many ways, I believe I also became that to him.

There was even one season in 2003-2004 when Randy had to head back to North Carolina to take care of some personal things with his family. When it came time for my training, he flew back to Orlando to make sure my training wasn't impacted by the real life issues he was going through. That is the very definition of a friend and a man dedicated to his craft.

There was a small window from 2008 to 2010 when I considered training on my own, but we stayed in touch, and I would still turn to Randy whenever I needed advice. Then, of course, after my injury with the Indians in 2011, I needed Randy in my corner as I tried to resuscitate my career. He immediately threw out the flag to let me know he was there for me, and I knew who I wanted to be involved with and who could best help me. We rekindled the fire and created my plan for recovery. We sat down, as we always had, to discuss the injury and the diagnosis of my knee along with the prognosis and our game plan for resurrection and recovery, and establishing our goals and objectives. We took it one day at a time. There were certain baby steps we would have to take toward progress, so Randy took me by the hand—without babying me—and he guided me through my recovery. He got me to do things I never thought I'd be able to do again after sustaining such a debilitating injury.

I was completely committed to coming back, and I would do everything I needed to make it happen. Randy really helped coach and manage me. With my motivation and drive to come back, I would have worn myself out without his guidance and ability to map out what needed to be done. In many ways, Randy saved me from myself and from my tunnel vision. He would occasionally need to call for a day off or shut me down after a couple hours in the gym by sitting me down and simply having a conversation instead of letting me work out.

I put everything on the line to come back, because I didn't want to be finished with the game and have people questioning what I had done with my career. I wanted to leave this game on my own terms, not when a medical mishap kicked my ass out the door. I felt I had something left in the tank, and I came to work with Randy even on days that I didn't physically have anything to give. The days weren't pretty, but with persistence and consistency, we achieved every single goal we set for ourselves—be it squats, running, jumping rope, or vertical jump. Everything we did had a starting point and a goal, and by the time I was ready for the tryout, I'd achieved everything that Randy had laid down for me.

We established a timeline with Sheff of what I needed to do and when I needed to do it. Then we put our nose to the grindstone to push through and be ready for the tryout at University of Tampa in January, from where I was ultimately signed with the Phillies.

Having Randy Hadley in my corner was far more gratifying than relying on a shot in the butt and bottle of PEDs hidden on the top shelf of my locker behind the toothpaste and the jock itch cream. I'll put my methods up against theirs any day of the week.

Our typical workout regimen over the thirteen years we've been together starts off with me throwing my first pitch with my dad over Thanksgiving weekend. Then I come back to Orlando, and Randy takes over with my throwing and conditioning. We often laugh about it, because Randy and I will throw anywhere we can. Sometimes it's in a parking lot or in an open field with grass up to our knees, where if you miss a ball you don't know if you want to reach down and grab it because you don't know what you're going to find. We have a job that needs to be done, and even though I'm a professional player working out with a professional trainer, sometimes conditions aren't ideal, and I have to make do with the circumstances.

Randy has often said that, though he respects me as a baseball player and as a pitcher, first and foremost, I'm an athlete. We have done workouts in multiple gyms, at Disney, and even on the beach where Randy has me do sprints or high knees in the sand. I do drills that help me become more athletic and multi-dimensional than your typical baseball player. We even play a different kind of volleyball to teach me other athletic movements. I'm a grinder, and as Randy has pointed out, if he gives me slow monotonous movements, he'll lose my interest, so he has to put challenges in front of me that keep me engaged.

Though I hate it, Randy even put a picture of a carrot at the top of the Jacob's ladder in his gym. It's a teaser of achievement as though something is just outside of my reach, as when I am constantly working, moving, and chasing, and it is right there in front of me, but I just can't quite reach it. Even though it becomes frustrating and tiring, I don't give up. I continue to literally and figuratively chase the carrot.

Randy has spent time with my family, and he considers the Grillis to be a part of the Hadley clan. My dad has occasionally spent time watching one of our training sessions, but Randy and I joke that Dad can't bring himself to stay through an entire session because they are so grueling. In fact, Randy said to my dad prior to our 2013 season, "Steve, if you thought they liked him in 2012, wait until they see him in 2013," which was perhaps a little bit of foreshadowing for what was to come for me and the Pirates during our magical 2013 season. When you hear my dad speak of Randy, he sounds more like he is speaking about one of his own children rather than his son's personal trainer.

Randy and I can talk with each other every day or once a month, and it feels just the same. We talk to each other and never miss a beat. As Randy says, "We don't always agree with each other, and sometimes don't want to hear what the other one has to say, but that makes for a very healthy friendship and relationship." I can honestly admit that during workouts, Randy isn't my best friend. Our expression is, "You don't like how it feels, but you love what it does." If I like him too much at the end of a workout, it means he's not doing his job; his job is to take me places I'm not willing to go. I had to learn to trust him and know he'll take me to the Promised Land if

I shut off my brain and follow his lead, drawing on that pain, that burn in my chest. I know he's going to get me to where I need to be. There are definitely days I don't like the man very much, but we're both okay with that.

One of my fondest memories is when Randy and I were driving through Florida and decided to take a ride on a roadside helicopter. We were driving down the highway and, on a whim, we took an exit, and the next thing I knew he had me up in a helicopter overlooking I-4. We were both nervous, but when you're with your friend, the thrill of the ride and the trust in each other overrides any sense of fear.

Like me, Randy is against PEDs. In an effort to compete against those who choose to cheat, baseball players are forced to become more athletic and use a more athletic approach to training, but that has always been the basis of Randy's training techniques. Randy laughs when people ask him how I am doing all that I am at this stage of my career. His answer is that I'm not doing anything differently than I've always done, I'm just getting the opportunity to use my skills in a different situation. Though our training routine has changed over the decade-plus that we've been together, our workouts have always been athletic-based. We knew it would never be a quick fix or that it would ever be an easy road.

Loving and respecting the game was what was taught to me, and having pride in beating those who were selling their soul to the devil was my motivation. Sort of like the David versus Goliath method, *The Little Engine That Could,* and the story of the boy with the chip on his shoulder, these inspirations and motivations drove me each and every day to achieve. Randy and I sat across from each other one afternoon and discussed the fact that using PEDs had crossed my mind as a way to come back and a way to even the playing field. He and I agreed that at the end of the day when I look in the mirror,

I wouldn't be happy with the choice I'd made and the repercussions that I would face if I were ever caught using them.

I try to play the game the way I was taught, with respect and love and a passion that fans deserve to see every time they witness the game played at its highest level. I pride myself on being a grinder and toeing the line, pushing myself with everything I have. The idea of putting my integrity and my reputation on the line for a quick fix is not something that would ever sit well with me.

It's a privilege every time I step on the field and stand on the rubber, and I hope that my adoration of the game is evident to everyone who sees me play. It made my decision to take the road less traveled an easy choice. I ask myself if the guys who choose to take steroids are showing disrespect to the game, and my answer is a resounding yes. Playing in the steroid era, I'm guilty by association. When the line was drawn in the sand, even considering everything I went through, I chose to remain true to myself and to the game. My numbers are my numbers. The numbers of those familiar names who tested positive for enhancement drugs defamed the game and stole records from the Hall of Famers who played the game before us. Their numbers are lessened because of the guys who didn't respect the game.

I am a proponent of testing for performance enhancers and will gladly pee every day if that's what they want me to do. There were those of us who weren't doing it and who wanted testing as a way to clean up the game and level the playing field. When you're sitting in the locker room next to a guy who is using and you're both competing for the same job, it puts you in a position to make tough decisions that you didn't think you'd ever have to make. I was coming back from two elbow surgeries and found myself competing against guys who used to throw 88 mph, and suddenly they show up at spring training throwing 95, so I understand what temptation feels like. But when I leave the mound at the end of the day and hang up my uniform for the final time, I'll know that the numbers on the back of my baseball card are the result of hard work, dedication, and a chance meeting thirteen years ago with a guy named Randy Hadley.

I love you, brother.

CHAPTER 12

JOINING FORCES WITH SHEFF

> *"I'm not one of those people who has to try and remember what he told people, because I always tell the truth. That should count for something, right?"*
>
> ~ *Gary Sheffield*

It was mid-July and I was at a Big League game in Miami to see the Marlins play the Nationals at Joe Robbie Stadium. It was ironic in some ways to be there with my son, as it brought me back to the place where it all began for me in my Big League debut against the Atlanta Braves. It was hard for me, and I had a couple of cries before the game even started. The parking lot attendant gave me my parking pass and said she loved me and that I was her favorite Marlin. That made me feel good, and as we pulled into the stadium to see the action, a nostalgic feeling hit me.

I didn't care so much about what was happening on the field, because I knew what was going on inside the locker room. I wanted to be changing into my uniform in preparation for my walk to the bullpen. You tend to take those long monotonous steps for granted.

There is a love-hate relationship that exists in the game. Many guys love the game the same way they did as a Little Leaguer, while others, like me, have to battle, showing that staying in the Big Leagues injury-free and putting up numbers is a constant battle for survival.

It was good to get as close as I was that night to the real feel of the game. The fire in my belly was still there, and I knew right then that I was not done. Not only that, but when I recall all the instances that led up to that point, it makes me realize why I wrote this book. I don't know that anyone will care about my story, but it is mine to tell and share with the most important fans of all: my kids and my grandkids.

The signs are in front of me everywhere I turn: from meeting Bree to hanging with Nate; from watching Anthony, a boy I met at Nate's comeback game, who is missing two legs and has to wear two prosthetics to play the outfield; and to the YMCA I'd just joined that has the inscription painted on the wall, "When life throws you a curveball...Crush it." Even seeing *How to Train Your Dragon*, where the kid winds up with a prosthetic leg. These things can't be made up, and are all part of my journey.

One night, Danielle came in crying as two of our friends, Nate Robertson and Mike Maroth, were without jobs. One was due to injury and the other because he was not pitching well and wanted to make some changes. The game can be like that and can change in a heartbeat. We were all together in 2006, celebrating our time in the sun by pouring champagne on one another after every series win, and now we are all treading water to try to stay in the game. This is quite different from the life of a regular worker, where you can sign on at twenty-one and often not have to leave until retirement day at sixty-five. For us, the shelf life can be three or four years in some cases, where you go from the top of the rollercoaster to the bottom of the scrap heap. Though I wouldn't trade this life for anything in the world, job security certainly isn't one of the fringe benefits that comes along with this career choice. Some of us have fewer worries than others due to contract status, while others may be out of a job after two or three rough days in a row. Much of the job security is also about being at the right place at the right time.

Ironically, I feel like I was in the best position out of the three of us, and yet in a season where there wasn't an abundance of available relief pitchers, I was out. I couldn't seem to time this right. Not to mention another team I was with was in first place. That is the running joke: I seem to miss a team's success by only a season. I'm on the Rockies' team, and they struggle. I leave and they catch fire. I'm on the Rangers' team and they struggle. I leave, and they are in first place. I know I'm not the reason, but I better not let the sabermetrics guys get hold of that stat, or I may never work again.

October 3rd arrived, and it marked my 81st visit to PT, which in baseball mathematics is the number of half a season of games. It's funny how numbers are such a big part of baseball. Everyone who follows the sport knows that 60' 6" is the distance from the mound to home plate, yet no one knows the size of a hockey net or a goal post. Numbers like 714 (number of homeruns Babe Ruth hit), 0.406 (Ted Williams' average), 61 (Roger Maris' home run record until Bonds passed it), and 42 (Jackie Robinson's number) are all part of the lore of baseball that makes it such a unique sport for the player, the fan, and the enthusiast. It's part of why I live and breathe the history of the game.

No telling how many days of my own PT at home and in between visits had occurred—likely too many to count. Does time matter anymore? It did that day as the 2010 regular season finally ended, and I was now on a level playing field with many players who were watching the playoffs from their couches, too. That is, if I can even muster up the excitement to watch. It is hard not to peek in on games now and again. Baseball can be a sickness that sticks in your veins, similar to what heroin addicts must feel when they need their next fix. I'm the same way. My addictive behavior burns within me, and I do not have a solid release for that part of my personality when I'm not playing. I was going crazy inside, and the frustration of having as many career days in therapy as I had relief appearances pained me.

I guess those days when I was all alone in my community's tennis court with no autograph seekers or kids yelling for a ball, I thought of how badly I wanted it. The fire in my belly burned so hot, despite all the hardships and feelings of frustration for not living up to my own expectations. As I fired each ball into the fence, I imagined a ghost hitter in the batter's box and thought of the movie *The Rookie*. There was no glory in what I was doing, as this is a part of being a professional athlete no one sees. It is a lonely place to be, but a necessary part of the game.

I again got caught up in the numbers of the game and realized that there were only eighteen weeks until the four greatest words in the English language are uttered: "Pitchers and catchers, report." I was the only baseball player in the world who was excited about spring training at that part of the year.

Through it all, there was a hidden blessing in all bad things. We never see the whole picture, and my faith has taught me that what I want right now will probably not be revealed until time passes—when God feels the lesson has been learned and the time is perfect. I have had the opportunity to see what life is like without baseball. The pressures of tight finances and feeling squeezed helped me understand how nice it is to have the luxury of five-figure paychecks and envelopes filled with meal money to be spent on road trips. The game has been good to me in so many ways, and I will try valiantly not to take things for granted.

I decided that, even if I were issued a number like 99 in camp, I would give every freaking hitter a battle when they stepped into the box. While I was experiencing mind-boggling amounts of pain, they were eating and drinking on a private jet, or munching on a giant bag of sunflower seeds while sitting in a Big League bullpen. Now it was time to turn the tables and allow them to experience three minutes of the hell that I'd experienced for the last ten months. My time was coming, and I had to be ready. I shifted my attention to a Balboa-esque regimen. It was my Rocky moment.

Texas advanced to the playoffs for the first time in franchise history in 2010, and the sting of the phone call when the team decided not to re-sign me after the 2009 season rang loudly in my ears. Texas management was so elated to get me in a trade the year before, and then they were so quick to have a change of heart because I was going to cost them too much money, being arbitration eligible for the second time. I couldn't help but feel envy and jealousy. I was happy for my teammates. They put in a lot of hard work to get to that point, but I was fueled by anger at not being a part of it. I really wanted a true opportunity that season, not quasi-pseudo-opportunities like I'd had up to that point. It was time to take a stand and move in a different direction with someone who understood what I was going through.

I had an appointment to meet with Sheff, a person whom I respect and with whom I actually played. Sheff had become a baseball-player agent, and he was referred to me through the grapevine. I felt Sheff might be a good fit for me, since I knew his history as a player, his bravado, and also the fact that people didn't realize he is a great businessman. I was strongly considering making the move, as I felt the Sheff/Grilli union would be representative of the attitude, the desire, and the ferocity of the new and improved me.

Sheff finished his career in 2009 at the age of 40, while hitting .276 with ten homers for the Mets. Perhaps one of the more interesting honors of respect for Sheff is that he was intentionally walked in his final MLB at bat. Despite being 40 years old and allegedly at the end of the ride, he still struck fear in opposing pitchers and managers. He had some offers to do some broadcasting for ESPN, but opted to take some time away from the game before doing anything else. When I called Sheff, who I played with and respected more than any other teammate, and told him of my situation, he agreed to come check me out in Orlando. Sheff said my knee didn't look good, and he wasn't sure if he wanted to put his name on the line with me as his first major league client. He had done some work with a series of minor-league clients, but I was to be his first big name.

Sheff estimated that I was at about 60 percent and only had about a 50/50 shot at making it back, but knowing the man I was, he took the next step and decided to get his agent's license and become certified to represent me as his first major-league client.

I wasn't foolish enough to think that an agent can get you a deal if you put up shitty numbers. You have to put the ball in his court to make that happen. He's an agent, not a magician, and if the numbers don't stand up for themselves, even the greatest player agent won't be able to pull a rabbit out of his cap. Sheff was the first person to tell me that I was abused as a player, and he could clearly see that. He felt that a player of my caliber should not have to scrape and claw to get a multi-year deal, or go every day not knowing if he is one bad pitch away from AAA. You never know who you can trust in this business, but somehow I felt Sheff was one of those few I could trust.

I was early to rise the next day and I'd just got back from a Balboa workout. Usually, my dog woke me and dragged my tired ass across my kitchen to let her out and feed her. That day, it was me who was waking the dog to get my revenge. She lay there all comfortable, dreaming sweet doggy dreams, while I slapped stuff in my bag a little louder than normal in order to wake her sorry ass. Payback's a bitch, bitch.

It felt good to be well-rested, because many guys were very tired, while I was refreshed. Watching the guys in the playoffs reminded me of the very reason I was waking early, as I knew it took many hours of hard work to reach that point. It is one thing to say you have the team to win it all in spring and then another to actually accomplish your goal between the lines. There has been many a paper champion in April playing golf in early October.

I was also going to visit with Sheff that day. My current agents at the time had not checked in with me for a while. I really would have liked to have heard a, "How are you doing? How are you feeling? How are things coming along? This is what we are doing for you." In this day and age, a lack of communication is unacceptable. A text, an email, a voice message wouldn't have been too much to ask. Your agent is supposed to be on your side, but unfortunately, I didn't feel like my representation had my best interests in mind. Again, the business of baseball is a cold and frustrating part of the game.

So I headed off to talk to Gary and his staff about how they could help me jump-start my career. They could not pitch for me, nor did I expect an agent to do me any favors. I wanted to give my agent all the ammunition possible to make my case solid. I felt a guy like Sheff—an old teammate who had negotiated many of his own contracts, even with George Steinbrenner—would be a good fit for me.

Sheff was still relatively new in the industry, and I would be his first Big League client. He had negotiated several $100,000 contracts for the minor-league players he represented. In some ways, Gary was taking a chance on me, just as I was taking a chance on him. I thought that, at the end of the day, we would both be more than pleased that we took the risk for each other.

I'd just finished watching the documentary entitled What the Bleep Do We Know?! It's a movie about exploring life's possibilities and how our emotions cause us to experience our own reality. It seemed as though a disproportionate number of instances had been placed in front of me, screaming to make sure I was paying attention. I even saw one such sign at the airport, where I witnessed a man in a wheelchair with a metal prosthetic leg. I was inspired to take notice of things that I once maybe missed, and because my senses were heightened, I was paying closer attention and not missing the breadcrumbs that had been sprinkled upon the trail. These were breadcrumbs that led me steadily back to the world to which I strived to return.

I next went to speak with my new powerhouse of an agent. He was so much in my corner that I felt doubly empowered. I wouldn't let myself down, and I surely would not let him down either. I'd never been in the presence of someone who would represent me in such a manner, and I knew that he believed in me. He wouldn't allow a team with which he was negotiating to take control of the negotiation or put a negative spin on a player's ability. Up to that point, no one who had represented me understood that any better. I look back now and know that this was a pivotal decision and the best one I could have made for my career.

I was then off to my last visit—barring something catastrophic—to Vail. It seemed crazy to think that, not long ago, it took me forever just to get to the bathroom in the very same hotel where I now stayed. Now I didn't even want to take the shuttle ride down to the Steadman Clinic, as I relished the joyous walk from my hotel to the rehab center.

I completed a killer routine, and Luke helped me finish one

more of his Britney Spears routines. I tease about Britney, because after my workout, my right ass cheek felt like someone chucked a spear into it. My right cheek domination can only translate into great things on the field. And if worst came to worst, I'd tell him I'd be able to do one badass rendition of "Baby One More Time."

On November 11, 2010, I turned thirty-four-years old—just another number—but hopefully an age considered to be my prime in the baseball world. Whether or not teams would view me as a Big League pitcher would be determined by a couple of things. It was critical to let teams know that I was healthy and ready to go. My arm and body were fresh and ready to take on another Big League season, but I didn't expect much interest from teams, seeing as how I'd missed a full season. I would once again have to prove myself. With names like Cliff Lee and Jayson Werth leading the parade of free agents, not many people would come after a guy who had three major surgeries and missed a full season. I wasn't going to lead a parade of free agents signing ridiculous salaries, but I knew I could be an important cog to help stabilize the backend of someone's bullpen. Plus, I saw myself as a character guy, a guy who could help teach important lessons to the younger guys and keep a team loose during the dog days of summer.

That is where the advantage of having a representative of Gary's caliber was crucial, as I felt teams would listen to him and trust what he had to say. Yes, he is an agent, and that can be a smelly word in this business, but I was confident that teams would not view him as the crooked, conniving, sneaky, snake-oil vendor, as some guys in the business are perceived to be by owners and GMs. With Sheff in control of the negotiation, people would listen. That was the reason I liked hanging around his locker to talk baseball and business when we both played for the Tigers.

Although he was much older and a future HOF-caliber player, I saw a lot of the same intensity in me as I saw in him. I was not into astrology, but maybe that behavior is a commonality of Scorpios. He is a straight shooter, and you cannot bullshit him. I like to think I'm cut from that same bolt of cloth.

Sheff told me that I was one of the few young pitchers he played with who wanted to learn the game from a hitter's perspective and wanted to get better every single day. "I admired that in you. You'd come to my locker every single day, wanting to improve and see the game through the batter's eyes," Sheff explained while justifying his decision to take me on.

He shared some things with me about my comeback, and I really listened intently and took his advice and his wisdom to heart. He shared with me how to pitch and how to attack hitters. He asked me which pitches I'm most comfortable throwing, and when I told him fastball and slider, he asked me why I threw my curveball. I told him that I use my hook to set up hitters to induce them to hit into double plays. He said, "You can't be out on the mound, all pumping your fist and beating your chest to get a ground-ball double play. You need to be the kind of pitcher who strikes people out and then does all those kind of things. I wasn't a hyper guy on the field just to hit singles. Your personality and your stuff don't match the results." He spoke to me almost like a father would lecture his son.

We talked a lot about my style and my demeanor on the mound. "If I saw a pitcher pumping his fist when I was hitting, I took it to mean that he was excited that he got someone like me out, so I was never offended by it. All I wanted was to do something about it. There is a difference between someone trying to show me up and simply having a style. I've always believed that if someone has a style you don't like, either stop it or do something about it. When people don't like things like shaking your fist or flipping your bat, they're a bunch of crybabies. No grown man should tell another grown man how to play the game." How could I not love this guy?

Sheff continued, "I don't have to act like you. I don't have to play like you, but that don't mean I'm a bad person. What people don't seem to realize is that everyone has their own way of doing things, and as I said, if you don't like it, stop it. Get behind what you are saying."

"You're too nice," he told me. "This is how I operate. If you don't like me, I don't like you. That's how I am. I don't come into a relationship disliking anyone in the world, but if you disrespect me, I'll disrespect you right back. But you, you're too nice, because you always accept what people do to you. Somebody may put you in a position that you don't like, and you accept it, even though what they are doing may negatively impact your career. And you accept it, and that's a no-no with me. Nobody is going to put you or me in a situation that we don't like without hearing about it. Until you start speaking up, ain't nobody going to respect you. One thing I never did in my twenty-three-year career was let people put me in a position that they thought was best for my career. They may not have liked me, but they respected me. I bet on me."

Sheff was teaching me that if someone puts me in a game and I don't belong in that game or it's not in the best interest of my long-term health and career, I needed to make sure they heard about it. Not to be disagreeable, but to confront those who may negatively affect me, instead of rolling over and playing nice. "This is your career," he admonished. "Nobody gets to do what they want to do with your career without you having a say in it. Where I'm from, that never happens."

Sheff forced me to look at things a little differently than I had up to that point. I didn't have to be confrontational, and the world didn't need to think any differently about me, but I needed to take control of my own destiny.

Sheff advised me to stick with my best and to challenge hitters more and go for the punch-out. Clearly, he was encouraging me to take care of business on my own without giving the batter a chance to control the outcome of the interaction. At that point, I all but abandoned the curveball and started using the inner top half of the plate more. In a nutshell, Sheff helped change my demeanor, prepared me to take the long-awaited trip to the back of the bullpen, and helped to make me the pitcher I am today.

He promised me that he would not only get me a job to be a closer, but predicted that I would have 25 saves at the All-Star break. It took me a couple of seasons to work my way into that role, but as most of my fans know, I reached that plateau in 2013, my first full season closing-out games. Sheff was convinced—and subsequently convinced me—that if I did my job, he would get me the job that I was supposed to have. That was the job of a closer and not a middle-of-the-game reliever. He and I both felt the only thing that stood between me and greatness was that I wasn't in the right role and hadn't been for my entire career. He felt that if I had been a closer my whole career, I would be entering my fifteenth year as a major leaguer and would not be fighting for major-league survival. To have a former major league player, not to mention a major league player the caliber of Sheff, is an invaluable advantage. Let's see Scott Boras stand in the box against one of his pitchers, telling him which pitch he would have hit for a home run, as Sheff did for me. With a guy like Sheff in my corner, there was no way I could fail.

I got a call to meet both him and Xavier James, a lawyer from Sheffield Management Team, at the Swan and Dolphin Hotel where the 2011 winter meetings were taking place. We ate dinner with several people, but I honestly don't recall who they were because the room was filled with all kinds of front office personnel. The introductions soon blended together, and I was merely trying to filter my thoughts in anticipation of what lay ahead of me over the next several days. I was amazed at the hoopla of the festivities, where many people were discussing rosters, key additions, and writing player contracts on cocktail napkins.

Sheff kept telling me there were several teams that were excited about me, and as teams saw me walking around the meetings with him, I started to feel as though things were going to work out better than I'd expected. I met several GMs, coaches, old teammates, and MLB scouts. We enjoyed dinner with some Yankee personnel, and it was obvious that Sheff was trying to create as much buzz as possible. His name carried more weight than mine, and I sort of felt like I was a prizefighter and he was Don King.

I had stepped on a rusty nail before spring training of 2010, blew out my knee and then cut my eye before the year's end. Things happen in threes, and following this trio of ominous events, I believed that three positive things were about to happen to offset my streak of unfortunate circumstances.

I was getting ready for Christmas with the family in Orlando. The freezing temperatures threatened my palm trees, so I tried to save them. (I'm not sure what all of this global warming chatter is about, Mr. Gore). I replaced those same palms the previous winter, following a long, deep, cold spell that put an end to the tropical scene around my pool. I looked at the entire backyard and chuckled to myself with disbelief. There I was spending money on tarps and blankets at a time when all players see their bank account dipping. I didn't have money to burn, yet replacing trees would cost a boatload more than tarps and blankets. They cannot wait until April 15th, when again I would start making a regular seasonal salary, instead of the off-season stipend that we get. No matter how much one makes, it is about what you are used to making.

With Christmas time arriving, all Danielle and I really needed was a pair of healthy legs underneath me, and with that, I got my wish. We were just hoping to enjoy the excitement of Jayse's second Christmas and a fun holiday season. I was healthy, but proving my arm was healthy would be my next obstacle to overcome. Sheff felt strongly that I had been set up for failure, due to how teams had used me.

That opinion meant a lot coming from a player like him. He shared what other players had told him while he was playing for the Yanks. I always seemed to fare well against them on baseball's biggest stage. He told me that players like A-Rod and Jeter told him, "This guy's tough and has some nasty stuff."

People's opinions about my stuff matters, and what I bring to the mound matters to me, especially coming from guys who are well-respected in the game. I feel the best compliment you can receive is one that comes from your peers. The baseball fraternity is close, and to get respect from both foes and teammates means more than getting kudos from the media or fans. Albert Pujols came up to me in the Rockies' weight room one time to let me know that he was surprised to see me wearing a Rockies' uniform, and he complimented me on what a battler I am. Arguably, he is one of the greatest players of my era, and his coming up to me and striking up a conversation to say how he respected that I always came at hitters with everything I had was the greatest compliment I had ever received. Sort of like Picasso telling me he likes the way I color. I've faced Pujols ten times in my career, and he only has a double and two singles to show for it. Not stellar numbers, but better than many who have faced the most-feared hitter in the game.

Sheff worked his magic and got many teams excited as we accelerated my workouts and got my arm to be in near-mid-season shape for a pre-spring-training showcase to eight of the teams. He stirred up interest from the winter meetings by spreading the word that I was throwing 95 mph again, and I was healthy. I knew that Sheff was putting his neck out for me, and I was not going to disappoint him or the two people I wake up with every day. Danielle and Jayse had been through a lot with me, and they deserved to experience some of the rewards that come with this job.

A lot of preparation went into the day, and it was time to air it out and lay it all on the line. After all the stalling and restructuring of my offseason and workout schedule, there was no more delay. When you are out of the spotlight for a full season and unable to play winter ball in Venezuela, it is important to trust yourself without being stupid. I'd had several conversations with Dr. Steadman and Luke. They felt strongly about holding me back when I was considering playing winter ball, but now it was different. They understood my situation and knew it was time to throw caution to the wind and let loose. I still wanted their blessing before I moved forward, and to hear they felt it was time to lay it on the line was all I needed. I'd made it. I overcame "a grenade blowing up in my knee," and now the same set of expert eyes and hands that pieced me back together told me to put the pedal to the metal.

I was ready to showcase myself as an experienced Big League pitcher to the scouts from all the big-market teams. My entourage that day consisted of Randy Hadley, my personal catcher and former catcher for the Indians and Reds, Eddie Taubensee, who came with me for support and the drive to the University of Tampa. I treated them both to a Jimmy John's sub to thank them for their time and for helping me out. I ate an entire large Italian sub (what would you expect?), so I knew I was calm and ready.

Warming up, my arm was live, and if they wanted to see velocity, they were going to get it. I was smart because I knew that I didn't have to legitimately hit 95 mph, but only close enough to it to impress them. They understood that I was not going to risk hurting myself in only my fifth bullpen session of the offseason. Chuck LaMar, the Phillies scout, came up to me to ask questions and pry a little to see how I was doing. Sheff told me before the workout that they were really excited about me and that I would fit nicely in their bullpen. The Nationals, Angels, Dodgers, Red Sox, Yankees, and Phillies were all there. They were each big-market teams with deep pockets and a history of winning in all cases, except maybe the Nationals. Gary created the interest, but they wouldn't have shown up and taken the time to come see me if they were not truly interested in seeing what I could bring to the plate.

I was certainly throwing well enough that day to know that I had to be close. No matter what the scouts and everyone else were thinking, I felt I'd won a small victory. Of course, there was a lot on the table financially that was contingent upon how things went this day, but knowing how good I felt and how easy I was bringing it was almost good enough for me. I was feeling free and easy, which was the result of knowing that I had done everything I could to get to that point.

I remember looking at myself in the mirror in that lonely hotel bathroom the night I tore up my knee, and now nearly ten months later, my worry and doubt had finally disappeared. That was a huge burden to carry every moment, night and day, since the moment I fell on my face in Goodyear. My legs were once again underneath me, and my arm was ready to go for a nice spin in fourth gear. I wanted so badly to start uncorking some pitches as hard as I could just to see my arm strength, but my control would not have been as good. After the fact, I learned that I was throwing 92 consistently. I was psyched because I knew that was what this was about: velocity. I was so pleased, and I left that parking lot with a huge weight off my shoulders.

Later that same week, after thinking that my showcase was enough to impress, I was asked to come to another audition for the Phillies in Clearwater at the Spring Training Complex. I was prepared, yet unprepared, as Sheff, Randy, and everyone involved agreed that I should take the rest of the week off since I had already done what was asked of me. The Phillies were hosting a pitchers mini-camp for some of their young guns, and they asked me to come back to pitch in front of the brass. Rubén Amaro, Jr., the GM, Rich Dubee, their pitching coach, and Charlie Manuel, the Phillies manager, were all present. This time instead of velocity, they wanted movement, and that is exactly what I gave them.

Watching a respected peer from my draft class as he tried to make a comeback gave me some confidence. I watched him from the bullpen area of the complex, and his violent motion and loud grunting every time he threw only drew attention during his side session. He, too, was trying to catch lightning in a bottle, but I hoped they would sign me. This was serious, since I was doing all this without any guarantees of signing a contract while putting myself at risk. When you have no insurance, you start thinking about how dangerous it is to put your body on the line. I felt that this was a risk worth taking.

I imagined that no one was watching me, and I was merely enjoying the feeling of pitching in a uniform on a manicured mound. It reminded me of when I took the mound early in Game 1 of the 2006 World Series. You get to that point where you have everything to gain and nothing to lose. I was figuratively on the biggest baseball stage in the universe with more eyes watching me than I could ever imagine. You have to put it on the line, because the world will only remember your name for two reasons: because you are very, very good, or because you are very, very bad. There was only one of these ways in which I hoped to be remembered, and that's how it turned out. I pitched one and two-thirds innings, no hits, no runs, and one walk.

My experiences in 2006 helped me that day in much the same way. I knew that not only had I grown as a person, but also as an athlete. I had too much left in my body to be done with baseball, and I know that baseball is not done with the Grilli family. We missed it and wanted it in the worst way. That day driving home, I felt like it was all going to happen. At that moment, the Phillies were the front-runner.

CHAPTER 13

PHINALLY A PHILLIE

> *"I will hold a candle til it burns up my arm, I'll keep taking punches until their will grows tired, I will stare the sun down til my eyes go blind, I won't change direction and I won't change my mind."*
>
> ~ Pearl Jam, "Indifference"

There are many people who would agree that going to the mailbox is the highlight of their day. Some look forward to the Victoria's Secret catalog or the next Netflix DVD from their movie selection queue. You go to the mailbox in hopes of a tax refund check or hoping that Publishers Clearing House has selected you as the big winner. Besides my World Series bonus check, the contract from the Phillies was by far the greatest mail I'd ever waited to receive, and the anticipation ate me up like a kid waiting for Santa Claus on Christmas Eve.

There were many letters, many presents that came, but the mailman delivered in a big way that day. I was expecting UPS or Fed Ex to ship my contract, but it arrived via regular USPS, just to sharpen the pins and needles a bit more. I opened the mail in the car while Danielle drove, and I rode with Jayse in the backseat. We were heading to hang out at Barnes and Noble to let Jayse play with trains as he loved to do.

I opened a large envelope as if it was a Willie Wonka Chocolate Bar and I was looking for the golden ticket. I knew what was inside, but just like on the day my injury occurred, I saw my whole life flash before me in that instant. It didn't even matter if it turned out to be a minor-league contract or split contract, I felt I'd already won, no matter with whom or where I'd end up going. I knew I was going to fill the role that a championship team needs by mid-season, and that was the reason they wanted me and the reason I signed the contract.

Just like picking Detroit when I was a free agent, there was a feeling about Philadelphia that seemed like it was the right fit not only because they were considered favorites to win it all, but also because of all that went on behind the scenes to get to that point. I was about to open an envelope that contained a professional contract from a team that arguably had one of the best pitching staffs in all of baseball history. After all that I had been through, I figured that I would likely go to a lower-echelon team not expecting to win much. Maybe a bottom-dweller that wanted to have me do the Crash Davis thing, with some young gun slinging prospects in an effort to catch lightning in a bottle. No, this was my turn to catch my own lightning. I'd always felt that I deserved a better fate than I'd had, and I felt confident that this would be my time to reap the benefits of hard work and perseverance.

I read the best words I had ever seen inked. There, on a Philadelphia Phillies letterhead, it said:

Dear Jason:

Welcome to the Phillies organization.

I am pleased to enclose your 2011 Minor League Uniform Player Contract for your signature . . .

With a lump in my throat, I envisioned my return to a locker with a jersey hanging in it—a jersey with my name and number on it—and my walk to the bullpen before game time. I fast forwarded my thoughts and tried to contain the excitement within me. Sure, I was excited to be drafted by the New York Yankees out of high school. Sure it was great to be a first-round pick by San Francisco. I came back from a broken arm and Tommy John surgery. But this... this was my third and most difficult obstacle to overcome up to that point. In baseball, you don't get four strikes. You get three, and then you are out. I now had a huge opportunity to ride out the rest of my career and end it better than I could have hoped. I finally believed this wouldn't be the end of my story, but just a chapter in the middle of the book.

With one piece of the puzzle in place, I was pumped to dive head-first into spring training in Florida, instead of Arizona, as it was with the Indians' camp. Being close to home was a huge plus. We lived close enough to run back to Orlando, but far enough away that we couldn't commute like I did when I was a Marlin or a Tiger. Two hours each way was a bit far to drive following a full workout in the spring heat. We needed to find a place to help me focus and to utilize my downtime, in order to give me every opportunity to make the club. There were to be no distractions nor any excuses in my quest to regain my position in a Big League bullpen.

Going into the weekend, we packed up and headed to Clearwater to look at the apartment of a relative's good friend. With a late signing, making living arrangements and keeping things budgeted until April 15th when paychecks started coming in again, this travel opportunity was perfect to give my family the peace of mind needed to enjoy spring training.

The apartment was more than we could have asked for. We had a marina- and gulf-view off the sixth-floor balcony. We were a stone's throw away from the beach. Walking 300 feet to the silky white sand of Clearwater surely would allow me some time to digest the adjustments in baseball life and fine-tune my mechanics in my head.

Walking around the beachfront town and seeing buildings with Welcome Back Phillies signs throughout the city was incredible. Bars hung banners. It really was getting exciting to be a part of that energy. I wondered, is everything going to be spelled now with a "ph" in front to make the "f" sound? Phantastic, I am phinally a Phillie. Holy phuck. This wouldn't be the last time we saw this happen.

It was eleven months to the day since my injury. I officially put pen to paper, signed my contract, and walked to my mailbox. At one point, that would have been a feat in itself. I had in my hand an executed contract and additional paperwork in a return envelope to send back to my new employer, team number eight, The Philadelphia Phillies. I felt on top of the world and was an ecstatic Phanatic for the time being. There would be no jersey unveiling or press conference announcing that I signed, but I didn't deserve that, nor did I want all that attention. I enjoyed the celebration with the two people who mattered most. They were the reason I woke up every day and kicked my own ass back into playing condition.

I am surrounded by baseball all over the place, and I have invested my life into this game. I am an outlier, an observation that is numerically distant from the rest of the data, yet an outlier who still had a chance to hang on to a dream that many have had. I was thirty-four years old, but I was filled with a new resurgence, appreciation, and love for the game. This was an accomplishment that would more than likely go unnoticed, but they have a Comeback Player Award every year, so why should it not be me?

I refused to allow any negativity to surround me during my recovery. This was a task that needed all things positive, and I had not allowed any negativity to enter my dojo. I even started tweeting motivational quotes every day in order to provide myself with positive brainpower to help overcome my injury. That was part of the healing process. If you conceive it and you believe it, you can achieve it.

Luke, my physical therapist in Vail, shared his excitement as he admitted that I must have been wearing a bulletproof vest, because I could not have asked for a better outcome. I remember hobbling around the grounds, trying to take in some fresh air and the frustration of being on the crutches that accompanied it. When something bad happens, time goes by slowly, and when you are having fun or enjoying the moment, life moves really fast. I may never throw a no-hitter, I may never accomplish something that is Hall of Fame worthy, but when I look at my copy of the signed contract sitting on top of all the paperwork on my desk, I am thankful for every moment of the entire experience.

I foamed at the mouth to step foot into the spring training complex. For as much as I love our home, I was ready to pack up what I needed to get going and leave that place in the rearview mirror for a while. I felt the itch for competition and, of course, the itch for a paycheck. We celebrated Valentine's Day the night before we headed to Clearwater, so Danielle knew how much she meant to me. However, I can confess now, in retrospect, that my mind may not have been on the celebration of love. My emotions were running wild, and I could not sleep at night, let alone play Romeo to my Juliet. I was so tired, but I relished the fact that I was in love with spring training.

No matter how much you miss baseball, you never like packing up for six months on the road or trying to close up your home. It's a very stressful part of the business. Those are the times when I wished I had enough money to just get new stuff when we arrived at our destination. It felt like today was yesterday, and yesterday was today. That is because it was. We left at 1:00 AM, rolled into Clearwater by 3:00 AM and unpacked.

I was signed by the Phillies, and even though I was trying to be optimistic, I knew it was going to be a long shot to make the team when they handed me number 93. They signed me to a split contract, meaning I was not assured a major-league visit and was not even a member of their forty-man squad. Much of my camp was spent on the minor-league side of the complex, as I only appeared in three games on the major league field. It was apparent at that point that the intent was to keep me as insurance, in case anything happened to one of the members of the Big League pen. When a system is as deep with major-league arms as the Phillies were, they begin to stockpile talent, and it was evident that I was just one head of cattle in their stable.

I was pissed, because when I signed, they said they envisioned me as that late-inning guy, but after appearing in only three games all spring and faring well in each, I was jettisoned back to the minor-league camp. My first outing was against the Yankees on the road, and I earned a save throwing nothing but cheese. After everything I had been through, there I was in a spring-training game, and yet it felt like the World Series facing New York and Big League hitters. I thought that appearance was going to put me on their radar as their seventh- or eighth-inning guy. There was a long while between appearances, and I spent a lot of time on long bus rides from split-squad game to split-squad game without getting off the pine. I'd get back to Clearwater, head back over to the minor-league camp, and the guys would ask me if I got in. More often than not, my answer was no, as I only saw four innings of action in thirty-two spring-training games.

When camp broke, I headed north, not as a Phillie, but as a

member of the Lehigh Valley IronPigs. During that period, I received a million-dollar offer to play in Korea, and I wrestled every day whether to stick it out in AAA, or take the money and play overseas. We were in Scranton, and I pulled my roommate Tagg Bozied into the laundry room and said, "I have to make a decision in the next five minutes, or the offer is off the table. What would you do?"

He said, "Grill, if you were struggling with a 5 or 6 ERA, I would tell you to take the money, pack your bag, and get out of here, but you are a Big League pitcher, you got a 0 ERA, and you're striking everybody out. It is clear you have Big League stuff."

Luckily, I had an out in my contract that stated if I didn't get a call-up, I could demand my release. After seeing a half-dozen guys called up ahead of me during the first three months of the season, I demanded my release, despite the fact that, in transaction writing, it says they released me, but that is because I asked for my release.

I had spoken with my former manager Clint Hurdle, who was now manager of the Pirates, and I'd told him what was going on. He had the Pirates send a scout to come see me when Lehigh Valley was playing in my hometown of Syracuse. The Pirates scout, Marc DelPiano, asked me if I could get an inning so he could watch me. I went and told my pitching coach what was going on, and they gave me an inning to showcase my stuff. I threw a clean inning, struck out a couple guys and then traveled to Pawtucket with the team. Sheff called me while I was there and told me he thought it was going to happen.

On July 21st, one day after I was granted my release by the Phillies, I was signed by the Pittsburgh Pirates and was reunited with Clint Hurdle, a reunion that ultimately changed the direction of my future. It marked the end of a journey that took me from the disabled list to the minor leagues and back to the majors with a first-place club. One day later in a game against our rivals, the St. Louis Cardinals, Clint gave me the ball in the top of the ninth of a game we would eventually lose 6-4. It marked the first time in the 473 days following my knee injury that I had stepped onto a major league mound, but it would not mark the last time that Hurdle would hand me the ball to start or end a ninth inning for the Pirates.

I had a great conversation with our closer Joel Hanrahan over a few drinks later in the campaign and got to know my teammate quite a bit better. We discussed the team's lack of experience and maturity and how it ended up costing us in the long run. We were 53-47 on July 25th and went 9-25 down the stretch. I tend to think we weren't as good as we really were on July 25th, and we aren't as bad as we are today, but as football coach Bill Parcells always said, "You are what your record says you are." I believe that being in too many close games can take its toll on a team, both physically and mentally. We were outscored 35-10 in a three-game series against the Padres at home in early August, and it really took the wind out of the sails of the Jolly Roger.

I was also badly missing Jayse and Danielle. My mood was snappy because I lacked the patience to feel like I could correct my family situation at home. Jayse was crying for me, and I found myself in a catch-22. I enjoy the travel that comes along with playing this sport, yet I wanted to be home so much at that time. I had worked so hard to get to where I was, and I was enjoying the hell out of it. I pitched well, and overall, I was healthy. I couldn't wait to fully recover and catch my breath during the off-season so I could get ready for more action the next season. I always felt spent and ready for the offseason. Then two weeks would go by, and the playoffs would be on, and I'd wish I was on one of the teams that were pouring champagne all over one other.

I was lucky enough to have a father/son workout with Jayse in the Big League stadium, and it instantly took me back thirty years earlier, when Dad and I played catch in MacArthur Stadium in Syracuse. I never really got to hang with Dad at a Big League park like Jayse does with me, but being inside a stadium throwing around the ball with your old man is as close to perfect as life can possibly get—shy of doing it in a cornfield in the middle of Iowa. All I worked for to have that moment was documented on my Flip camera, and it made my day worthwhile.

I also got to know more about my teammates as the season continued. I shared my story with 2010 All-Star Evan Meek and Daniel Moskos in the bullpen, after Meek asked me about my career. Meek actually had a tear in his eye. He was clearly taking Big League life for granted. Ironically, Moskos was the fourth pick in the draft in 2007, and now, half a dozen years later, he was fighting hard to stay in the Bigs. If this story doesn't sound familiar, please start over on page one and re-read. I shared my story with them during the game, and then got dry humped (when you get up in the pen, get ready to be used, and are then told to sit down again) again. It's the bullpen equivalent to being used and abused.

At this point in our development as a team, no one was taking us very seriously. Our accomplishments were overshadowed by the larger market teams who find themselves amongst the baseball elite year in and year out. This core group of guys continued to develop its identity. It was clear that there was enough talent to win, but winning is more than just assembling talent. It takes maturity as a team and time to develop the bond that comes with experience playing as a unit.

After getting a Japanese massage from some of the Rockies' therapists while in LA at the Langham in Pasadena, another pitcher, Chris Resop, joined me and we spent a good part of the evening kibitzing about what goes on in the "Burgh." I had been trying to figure it out and not remain silent about the issues that troubled the team. I was sick of just hoping that I would be playing somewhere competitive and watching how many opportunities slipped away. It was time to change the culture there and see if we could make Pittsburgh competitive.

After Resop left, I made a list of things I thought could help. It was difficult to step right in and say too much, because I feel that respect has to be earned, not just requested. I wanted to earn the respect of the team of which I had become a part. I had to be careful not to overstep my boundaries by getting up on a soapbox and expressing my thoughts and opinions too firmly. You earn respect and a platform by producing, and then and only then do you have a voice. My motivation to win was driving me to make the necessary improvements there, because I had witnessed so many times what it is like to be at the bottom, and I knew we could be better than that.

There is not much about Dodger Stadium that can excite you, other than playing Pac-Man in the clubhouse and the outstanding water pressure in the shower. The clubhouse is small and old. The field is legendary because of the history there, but the amenities are horrendous. Before we got to the stadium, Coach Dean Treanor baited me and challenged me to break my own legendary Pac-Man record of 158,000. I focused and chomped at the bit all night. I hate when people tell me I can't do something. I've made a career of trying to prove people wrong, and whether it's baseball, Pac-Man, or trying to get toothpaste back into the tube, tell me I can't do something, and I'll find a way to make a liar out of you. Not only did I break the record, but I shattered it by amassing an all-time Pirates' record of 200,000 points. Take that, Treanor. They told me I wouldn't run again, either, so I went after my Pac-Man dominance and was running around the field as Moskos and Locke were just getting to the park.

They told me they had already heard the news because everyone was watching me play Pac-Man at high speed, and they were amazed at my ninja skills. Half the team didn't even know about Pac-Man since they were not even born when Pac-Man was king, so I revealed my age once again. Locke and Moskos later said they had chills seeing me in full stride, enjoying a run around the field, knowing my story. Once again, I was just trying to lead and inspire by example.

The next day, I had a power lunch with a local entrepreneur who presented an opportunity I considered latching onto as an option for my life after baseball. I thought back to recent days in Lehigh Valley and realized how much life had changed since these opportunities aren't presented to IronPigs. The highlight of my weekend was getting Hall of Fame broadcaster Vin Scully to autograph a ball for me. One of my favorite Vin Scully quotes is, "Good is not good when better is expected." Doesn't that summarize the culture change that we were hoping to promote in Pittsburgh?

During a 15-1 late-season loss to the Dodgers, the phone rang, and I answered as if pizza and wing orders were being placed. Antonio's Pizza was born that day. I was hoping to keep the guys loose in our foxhole by talking about Antonio's in Pittsburgh, the most popular pizza spot on the planet. The goal was to keep it light, so as not to get too uptight watching a two-touchdown beating through the scratched fiberglass window of Dodger Stadium. Hopefully, the trend would continue into the next season, while also preventing us from losing our minds in the pen this late in the season.

We then traveled to Arizona and didn't fare much better there, losing two of three to the Diamondbacks. I hated the dry heat, but after that ass beating, I told the guys to meet me at the Merc Bar near the hotel. Fifteen guys and some staff joined us there, and we had a great time. It was what was needed—to hang out together more outside of the field. There was bonding going on, and it didn't matter if it was late in the season. We were creating a culture toward the next season, and hopefully the guys would finally get it, and carry it on. It was important to apply the rituals that I was exposed to on other teams on which I had played. If you bond off the field, then when you are in the foxhole and when personal issues occur, you bond on the field, too.

The journey was tough, and despite a less-than-stellar record for the team, my season had a happy ending because I made it back and stuck it out. We ended the season at a disappointing 72-90, but fifteen games better than 2010 and with a lot of good habits to build upon. I ended the season at 2-1, with a 2.48 ERA in twenty-eight games with the Pirates, and I had thirty-seven strikeouts in thirty-two innings. It was a lifetime better than 2010 and miles away from my journey to Goodyear, Vail, and Lehigh Valley.

CHAPTER 14

FOUR GREATEST WORDS IN THE ENGLISH LANGUAGE

> *"Champions aren't made in gyms. Champions are made from something they have deep inside them—a desire, a dream, a vision. They have to have the skill and the will. But the will must be stronger than the skill."*
>
> ~ *Muhammad Ali*

No one can ever question my heart or commitment to my craft. I may have been thirty-five and going into my fifteenth professional season, but I still had a lot to prove and work hard for. Had I not had all of the ups and downs that I was forced to endure, then maybe spring training wouldn't have been such a treat. Most guys hate spring training, as it marks the end of hunting, vacation, and free time, and it extends the already long season by two months. With each new season comes the realization that the game hasn't yet gotten the best of me, and I'm ready to slay the dragon once again. Every February is more special to me than the one before, and there is no doubt in my mind that the four greatest words in the English language are "Pitchers and catchers, report." The forthcoming spring training surely would be more special than the last and maybe even the most enjoyable one of my career.

As spring training came together, it was pretty clear that Hanrahan was to be the closer, but I kept climbing up and was in line to be the set-up man. I couldn't help but think back to the conversation that Hurdle and I had in right field upon my arrival in Colorado, and true to his word, he was giving me the opportunity I sought. Different place, different situation, but the man came through for me, and I certainly will not let him, the team, or myself down. I, of course, avoided the shuttle run at all costs and nearly threw up at the thought of even considering it.

My career was back on track again, and I couldn't remember the last time I was so relaxed and able to clear my mind of all stresses. Who knew that Bradenton/Anna Maria Island would have so much to offer us and allow me to rejuvenate my soul and passion for all I had to accomplish? We rented a beach house one block from the beach, and it was worth every penny.

I was extremely focused, and my spring was as good as I'd hoped, since I put in my deposits from this past offseason and throughout spring training. The adrenaline rush came in my best moment of the spring during a night game versus the Orioles. I came in with runners on first and second and no one out. After getting a ground ball that turned into an error, I punched out two guys and escaped the inning only giving up an unearned run. It was only a spring training game, but they say you play the way you practice, and this inning was indicative of what I was capable of doing.

I ended spring with a total of 11 IP, with 2 ER, 7H, 1 BB, and 13 Ks between major- and minor-league innings. More important than the stat line was the mood of the 2012 Pirates' camp. I would summarize things as optimistic, with the organization putting everything in play from the physical and the mental side of things. We had meetings and PowerPoint presentations galore. I believe it was because manager Clint Hurdle was a great mentor and an outstanding speaker. If you go into his office, there is always a new book on his desk. I feel that all this meeting stuff is because today's player does not sit around and talk baseball after the game is over. There are too many other distractions, like iPads, iPods, the race to get home, no beer in the clubhouse, and so on. The good old days are over now and are likely never to return.

For the first time since I could remember, I had some gravel road eliminated and replaced with some freshly paved asphalt. I remember this feeling all too well, and I will never forget how quickly life can do a 180-degree turn on you.

I was entering my sixth year in the majors, which is a critical year in terms of service time. As a free agent after the season, it was what the players before me had fought so hard for—what Curt Flood did to set the wheels in motion back in 1969 when he refused a trade to the Phillies and fought the system to declare himself a free agent. Reaching six years of service time is the achievement of a milestone that could set up my family for the rest of my life. Sure, it was happening far later than expected in my fifteenth season of pro ball, but I had attained it nonetheless.

The best things I took away from that season came from my peers and coaches. The respect I earned was the best compliment I took away from the game. No matter the stats or how much money I made, I hope that my children read this one day and realize none of that matters if people do not respect how you handle your business. Being a consummate professional is something my father instilled in me. The old school ways are what I appreciate about growing up with a father in the game.

Pirates legend Kent Tekulve and Tom Filer, the AAA pitching coach, each told me I stood out in how I went about my business, and that this was good for the other rookies and younger guys to see. I was having a blast and was the loosest I had been in seasons. I tried to make others around me laugh, even if it was at my expense. I was trying to get the guys to unite as a team. Team dinners, social sparklers, and other impromptu get-togethers go a long way in shaping the make-up of the team. I couldn't do it alone, and I didn't want to be too much of a rah-rah type of guy. I think it is more important to have the team do as I do, not do as I say.

Dad came down to camp, as he always does, and we had a great time. I loved seeing him in his element and the rise it gave him. I don't know anyone who loves the game of baseball more than he does. A.J. Burnett shouted out to our traveling secretary when he was passing out our meal money, "Hey, Johnson. Mr. Grilli's here so much, don't forget his envelope." Joking around with the guys makes him feel like he is a part of the entire experience.

I sat alone in my spring training rental place thinking of my family and my competitive drive. I knew I wanted to work hard, because I loved it there so much. I wanted a piece of the island, and I could have it if I worked hard enough and long enough. If Jamie Moyer can pitch until he is forty-nine, then my journey is far from being over.

The last day of camp somewhat ironically falls on April Fool's Day. The team was not completely set, and breaking camp is always tough when you see guys who are right there until the end, then they get cut for different reasons. Daniel McCutchen and Brad Lincoln were two casualties on the year's list of victims. McCutchen didn't take it too well for good reason. He was a gamer for seventy-four games in 2011 and had good numbers, despite being abused out of the bullpen, throwing eighty-four innings. He'd had a bad spring, and he seemed to get frustrated with each bad outing he had. No matter what he was told in that office, I believe that the easiest route for management to take was to send out guys with options. I get filled with fire when people are not up front with others. It is just the way the business is done. No one wants to give that kind of news. Not with what is at stake. Families are involved, and income is a lot different between a Triple-A guy and a Big Leaguer, this year especially with league minimum now up to $480,000 in the majors.

I felt bad saying goodbye to quality people like those guys, but there is nothing that I could say to make it better. I had been victim of this scenario many times. Circumstances like that toughen the skin, hopefully for the better.

After finishing spring games in Florida with a much-needed victory over the Blue Jays in Dunedin, we boarded our Delta Charter to Philadelphia to close out the spring schedule. It was refreshing to see rookies and many guys who will never see the Bigs (or get their cup of coffee) get so excited to experience a taste of the Big League life. After seeing what McCutchen and some of the other guys went through, it was a nice change of pace to help ease that ill feeling about the sport.

It was also a nice feeling to drive past Bright House Field in Clearwater, where I trained in spring of 2011 with the Phillies. Passing that forsaken parking lot served as a reminder of how pissed I was about getting sent to Lehigh Valley, instead of going north with the Big Leaguers. Parking next to that garbage dump pissed me off every single day that I was not a major league player, but today I was a visitor, and once again, I was a card-carrying member of a Major League Baseball opening-day roster.

Many of us met down at the bar once we got settled. I bought the first round of drinks and wondered if many of the rookies and guys we brought along on the road trip would join us for dinner. It felt good to know that I was now the veteran taking care of the young guys, much like the older vets did for me when I was a kid. It was finally my turn to repay and pay homage to the fraternity of which I am a part. Todd Jones was a former teammate who I became great friends with, and he took care of me when I was cutting my teeth. It felt good to pay a small favor back to those who are now in the same position I once was in.

We took the guys to dinner at a great steakhouse called Del Friscos around the corner from the Ritz Hotel. Most of these guys had never ordered an after-game meal where MP was written on the menu next to the food's price column. Meek and I discussed that we would split the bill and take care of the guys at our table, as the two of us were to make $2 million combined. Nonetheless, it was great to see a guy order the most expensive dinner on the menu, and when they brought out a five-pound lobster tail, the kid was sweating. I knew he was thinking, *I'd better eat all of this shit.* The next day I nicknamed Ryan Beckman "Lobster Bisque."

Getting to the ballpark was such a great feeling. I was scheduled to pitch the fifth inning and face the bottom of the order. Running out of the bullpen was a great feeling. I had reached a point in my career where I was not fazed by much, and the peace of mind was priceless. There was no more grinding my teeth or losing my hair; it was finally time to do what I was destined to do. The first batter I faced was Carlos Ruiz, who grounded out to third. Then some speed demon bunted for a base hit that was perfectly executed. Jim Thome pinch hit after he received a standing ovation, and I was able to quiet the crowd by punching his ticket. I respect that guy so much for who he is and what he accomplished during his lengthy career, but it was pretty awesome to feel like I picked up where I'd left off the season before. I then registered the last out with a lazy fly ball to center.

It's always a treat to get text messages from my wife and my father, who are into every single pitch of every single game in which I appear. Many messages come through during the course of a game, and it is always fun to share what I am doing. This was the biggest year of my career. It was one I'd long awaited, and it was filled with hope and promise. Though I see guys getting paid big-time contracts—like Matt Cain at $112.5 million and Joey Votto at $225 million—I know that I will never so much as sniff that kind of money, but I was still in good company.

Walking through the streets of Philly, I gave a rebel yell without missing a beat, and I embarrassed a few of my teammates who just kept walking. I laughed so hard because the street performer playing electric guitar did not miss a beat either. The excitement caused by the end of another spring training caused me to spontaneously let out another rebel yell as I sang "Whole Lotta Love" by Led Zeppelin in the chairlift, which provided great acoustics. The chairlift is a handicap-accessible seat that mysteriously resides between the two bullpens at Citizens Bank Park.

My only hope was that my wife and son would arrive, in one piece, in Pittsburgh the next day. I couldn't wait to get settled and enjoy the experiences with them. Jayse was ready to get out of Florida and settle in Pittsburgh, and it might be the last time he could enjoy an entire season with Dad since he would be starting school in the fall. I wanted to savor the time with them as much as possible.

I enjoyed a celebratory drink on the plane on my way to the Burgh, after having a great spring that ended with a 2.45 ERA. Now it was time to go to work, as the next six months counted toward my next negotiation session.

Opening Day in Pittsburgh ended with a 1-0 loss to the Phillies, with their ace Roy Halladay outdueling our opening-day starter, Érik Bédard. On paper, this wasn't much of a matchup, as Bédard has won fewer games in four years in the American League than Halladay did in his last year with the Phils, but as they say, games aren't played on paper, and Bédard held his own.

I have morphed into the role of one of several bullpen leaders, which comes from conquering the many things I'd faced. It's pretty amazing that I was viewed as one of the leaders, considering I've never enjoyed being a soapbox type of guy. I believe that leadership comes through experience; it doesn't just come with age. I have become the voice that everyone seems to look for when the chips are down. That's what it's like in baseball. When you're winning and everything's good, it's an easy game to play, and anyone can play the part of the leader. If you're losing, on the other hand, guys turn to you to keep them loose and pick them up. It's not a role you sign up for, but more of a role that evolves. When a guy or the team is starting to lose confidence or get out of sync, it takes a guy with experience to pull his teammate aside and reel him back in. I never envisioned that I would fill such a role, but there I was with guys looking to me for guidance.

Yogi Berra said, "It's déjà vu all over again" and I got to experience the true meaning of that when I again faced Thome in Game 2 of the 2012 regular season. This time it was for real, but much like our last meeting in Philly, I punched out the veteran. I had a successful inning striking him out while he was getting a hometown welcome from the crowd. The "I don't give a shit" attitude was working, and I loved it. I'm cool and calm on the mound and in the pen, and it continued to create the desired results. Not to mention, that inning showed Philly once again that they screwed up trying to bury me in AAA the year prior.

We took two of three from the Phils, and then we were off on one of many road trips for us that month: LA, San Fran, and Arizona. I was so glad to be getting this out of the way. I hated LA, and where we were stationed at the hotel was in beautiful Pasadena, but was way the frick out in East Bumple Fuck away from everything. So the decision was whether to pay a $15 cab fare to go get a $15 breakfast, or just stumble downstairs to eat at the restaurant in the hotel.

One night later, I was tagged with a loss to LA on their home opening night. I served up a bomb to Ethier after having electric stuff. I was calm about it just the same. I felt like the sun shines down on a dog's ass some days. I was blazing 94-96 mph heaters and threw a Bugs Bunny slider that day, punching Ellis and Kemp out on three pitches each. A reporter for LA came up to me and said he had not seen Kemp look that bad—ever. I just simply said that I had a great slider, and it just so happened that Ethier took me deep. Sometimes you get the bear, and sometimes the bear gets you.

I was about to head up to the room, but decided to have a few beers and I'm glad I did because I got to hang out with Soundgarden minus their front man, Chris Cornell. I would not have been able to speak if he had been there, as the dude simply rocks.

We left LA with a bad taste in our collective mouths after dropping three in a row to Dodgers. Some days the pitching is strong while the hitting struggles, and the next day it seems to be the reverse. It would be interesting to see what unfolded there, because it seemed like an exact reenactment of our struggles in 2011. The pitching was pretty solid, but our hitting faced some stiff competition. We needed to find a way to manufacture some runs, otherwise it would be a very long year.

We went 7-8 in our next fifteen against the Giants, Diamondbacks, Cardinals, Rockies, and Braves, and we ended April with a disappointing record of ten up and twelve down. However, I started my fifteenth baseball season going for the jugular.

I ended my evening sitting in front of the TV, hoping to see the baseball highlights of the day, but as had become commonplace, the broadcast was inundated with negative baseball-related news surrounding players' past use of PEDs. When the sport I loved was shrouded in a cloud of negativity, it made me want to abandon my habit of ending each day watching the day's amazing plays.

CHAPTER 15

DOING IT FOR BREE

---///---

> *"Never give up. If anyone says, 'No' or that 'You can't', then push harder and prove them wrong. If you try your hardest and never give up, you'll never have anything to regret."*
>
> ~ Bree McMahon

During the Braves' series, having Bree and her boyfriend in attendance was a career highlight that evoked the human spirit and emotion that I put into every damn thing that I do. It was a moment I will never forget. Bree was attending college in North Carolina, and it was a perfect opportunity to bring her to a game. I cannot put into words what a wonderful friend and source of inspiration she was to me, and I am sure that we will remain friends forever. She always shows up at just the right time on days I need her most. Whether it's an unexpected text or phone call, it's as if God put her in my life to watch over me and to provide me with strength whenever I am weak.

I viewed Bree as an angel who walked through the door of the training room that day for the mere purpose of helping me gain perspective and get through my shit, and, in turn, she views me in much the same way. She says often that we pushed each other, and she doesn't think that either of us would be where we are today without the push we gave each other. We pushed each other and called one another out when one of us was slacking. Our relationship grew to one of not only training partner and mutual mentor, but to that of big brother/little sister. To this day, we still text each other when one of us is feeling down, and we somehow magically raise each other's spirits with a single word, text, or phone call. We still feed off each other nearly three years after we first met.

Bree ended up playing goalie for the women's soccer team at Brevard College in North Carolina. Once a highly recruited, college-caliber player at nearly every position on the field, Bree adapted her game to that of a keeper, where she obviously has to be quick, but didn't need to run the field like she once did. Her coach, Shigeyoshi Shinohara, fought valiantly for Bree, to make sure she kept her scholarship, and he grew to mean the world to Bree. She shared with me that he "won't let anyone put me on a pedestal and understands that, though I have my limitations, he treats me just like everyone else and deflects unnecessary attention from me, because he wants everything to be about the team and not one individual."

In a follow-up interview, Bree said, "My right leg will never be the same as it was, but I make the best of what I have. You can't change things. It is what it is, and you just have to make the best of it." She has undergone twenty-plus surgeries, and there is no end in sight, based on her decision to play the sport she loves. The strain and wear that soccer puts on her will ultimately decide her fate of subsequent surgeries. There is ample scar tissue in her good knee, so that when she bends, it sounds like a school kid cracking her knuckles in study hall. Each time the tissue builds up as a result of playing soccer, she will have to again make a date with the surgeon's knife.

Following the Boston Marathon bombings in April of 2013, Bree traveled to Boston and spent some time with one of the victims who lost a limb and the victim's sister, who was also injured in the attack. She went to offer support and share her wisdom regarding what it is like to go from able-bodied to disabled in the blink of an eye. She spent the day with them, then Skyped with another person who was injured in the bombing. "The families really appreciated it," she told me. "Seeing someone else who has gone through it made them realize that everything is going to be okay. They learned it's not the end of the world." So it's easy to see why this amazing young woman has had such a profound effect on my recovery and my life.

Meek asked me what the heck was wrong, as I appeared deep in thought on a night when I knew I would get into the game against the Braves. I told him that I was fine, but inside I was really about to explode. I wanted desperately to do well and perform for a girl who gave me more than I could ever give back to her in return. It was critical for her to see me not only enter the game, but to excel, so that she would know, without a shadow of doubt, that she was hugely responsible for getting me back to that point.

All I could hear in my mind were the words she uttered at lunch, that she was so happy where she was at in life right now, after almost losing her life and scarring her full physical beauty. All of that happened to this wonderful young woman, and, for her to have no bitterness is most astonishing of all. Despite the pain she still contends with on a daily basis, and despite dealing with a handicap that will not go away, she remains upbeat and positive. The least I could do, I thought, was reward her for her perseverance and her positive spirit.

I paced back and forth in the pen until it was nearing my time to get into the game. I walked to the backend of the bullpen and started puking. I was ready to fight like never before. I had never felt such emotion come over me. After I puked, there was this warm feeling that came over me in the third inning—two innings prior to my normal stretching time. As much as I felt like a bull in a china shop, I was able to calm my internal engine after the bell rang, signaling me to start my in-game routine.

The ball was blazing out of my hand. This was the feeling of invincibility that you rarely feel. People call it *the zone*. If that is what came over me, I was in it, and it could not have come at a more appropriate time. I warmed up and felt like the ball was coming out as crisp as my body would allow. There was little force to it, and it was a thing of beauty.

That night, the hitters got a taste of what the people and things inscribed in the dirt stood for. TM, CG, JJ, and † were all out there on the mound with me. There was nothing that night that could have stopped me, not with Bree in the stands. It was emotionally and physically draining as I punched out Uggla, Heyward, and Ross on fifteen pitches. I was Nolan Ryan-esque. With the last one, I pumped my fist and looked up at Bree, who was smiling ear-to-ear and cheering wildly.

I had a few days to live on that high, and was truthfully glad to have that time to recover. It shook me to the core, physically and emotionally, but was glad I had a happy ending to share with a person who was so special to me. I am proud to know Bree and share in her success of coming back from major hardships.

The only bad outcome from Atlanta was that my buddy Evan Meek was sent out to AAA. The business side of things crept in on him, and I had to do some of the consoling for him that was done for me the year prior. I knew he would return, but the irony of the gravel road was staring at me. To see what I went through last year was hitting close to home again, and it bit me indirectly. Losing Meek to the minors was a reminder to keep fighting the good fight.

They say April showers bring May flowers, and for us, May is the month that hitters start trying to get even. I was having one of those nights. A.J. Burnett had an outing when he tried to man up and take, despite the fact that he wasn't pitching well. I learned a lot about that guy that night and my respect for him grew exponentially. I loved the guy before, but after that I had no doubt in my mind that this was the type of guy we wanted to go to battle with.

We all were trying to figure out who would get their chance to get us through the rest of the ballgame, as it was a very long game. I got an inning—the eighth—but in a losing effort. These are the games in which you must be smart, since your level of concentration and plan of attack changes from what has occurred in prior innings. My strategy worked, but my curveball didn't. I was not going to hang anything, nor keep the ball down. That was where I saw everything being located, and every ball was finding a gap or flying out of the park. I wanted no part of that, and escaping an appearance by putting up a zero was a huge accomplishment. I kept the ball up in the zone, and after getting the first two outs, I walked two and gave up a hit to load the bases. With the pitcher coming up, I was not giving in, and I punched him out to end the inning on a nasty in-the-dirt slider.

So as May began, we were still trying to find our identity as a unit. It would be interesting to see where the page turned from there. It would be great to get off the road and be home with family in Pittsburgh. I was hopeful that we could regroup and get to enjoy the comforts of home field and home base.

After a sleepless night when I was deep in thought, listening to Chris Cornell's *Songbook* album, I opened one eye and saw 5:30 AM on the clock. I guess the emotional weekend in Atlanta with Bree had a lot to do with my restlessness. It took a lot of out me, and I felt emotionally hung over. My alarm came up quick, and after about three to four hours of sleep, it was time to go to the field after that hellacious beating the night before. I knew it would be huge if we could bounce back and pull out a win after dropping two to the Cardinals. And lo and behold, we did. I also got in again. I was a little too pumped up and was fighting the urge to not overthrow. My breaking pitch was not as sharp as it was the past couple of nights, but I got the job done. I know my limitations, and I worked with what I had that day. Despite a walk, I got two more tickets punched, including a big one on Carlos Beltrán. We set a team record for strikeouts in one game with seventeen as a pitching staff. It is always cool to be a part of the small stats, though they are only a sidebar to the real purpose of what we were in this for. Records are great, but winning and giving your all is what really matters.

We got a 6-3 win and prepared for a good flight home. Hopefully, the boys would figure out how good we were. The talent was there, and the current roster was so strong that I knew it would be magical to be one of ten teams that would head to playoffs. I knew Pittsburgh would be set ablaze, including the rivers, if we did make the postseason.

Going home for a bit would do us good. We needed to settle in and get off the torrid road schedule we had been on. Plugging back into home life seemed exciting and would help suppress the loneliness that filled me. Despite the free time on the road that I enjoy, it's a delicate balancing act of enjoying freedom while missing the ones you love.

Chris Cornell had me with "It's an All Night Thing" and "The Keeper," and helped me get through the battle with only a few hours of sleep. Pitching with adversity became what I did best.

We split ten of twenty over the next three weeks of May, with an even number of ups as downs, before winning five of six against the Cubbies and Reds to close out the merry, merry month of May. On

May 31st, we sat at twenty-five up and twenty-five down. They say a tie is like kissing your sister, and though I have the best female sibling I could possibly think of, that's not a place I ever hope to be. We were hoping to jumpstart the season as we entered June to create some momentum. I was sitting at 1-1 with a miniscule 1.80 runs against and twelve holds. I'd fanned thirty-five batters out of the eighty-two I'd faced, or 15.8 whiffs every nine innings. I know it's only a two-month sample, but if I extended it over a twenty-seven year career, I'd be Nolan Ryan. Now that's what you call *hyperbole.*

We opened June with two of three against Milwaukee and then had an off day in Cincinnati, a place I vaguely seem to remember. Rarely do places on the road have meaning, and all seem to blend into one. I was at a movie-plex trying to unplug and take some me time, when I came to find out I was actually in Kentucky. That's not a good thing when you not only don't realize what town you're in, but you don't even have the state right.

I had just shut my eyes after slamming pizza and having some quiet time, when I was summoned to a team social at a karaoke bar. The fellas said it had my name written all over it, and I couldn't let them down. I sang, to my amazement, without any drinks in me, and made damn sure that famous-yet-infamous "Rebel Yell" was heard by all in the vicinity of Riverfront Stadium. It didn't matter now if they were in Ohio or Kentucky, they were going to know that GrillCheese was at the mic. It seemed like team continuity was happening, and it was cool to see they got me to come and hang out—something I was hoping would occur—and it was nice to see it all coming together.

I was having a blast so far in the season, and time was flying by. I tried my best to absorb my thoughts and emotions, and I came to the realization that the gravel road seemed to be smoothing. The Associated Press had a great article on me that I hoped would only help me in consideration of the All-Star game.

Danielle and I had a newborn on its way before spring training, and that gave me incentive to continue to pitch my balls off. My time was now, the moment I'd been waiting for. Everyone seemed happy, content, and blessed. I was trying not to take it all for granted or make any wrong moves. It was like hanging a breaking ball.

The feeling of anticipation of things ahead on the horizon was so great. I had been really good at problem solving. That is what I do for a living, only it happens on the baseball field. Somehow, it now felt like that ability also translated into everyday life. Whatever comes my way is likely to be a challenge and a testament to the journey that I have been on. I was relishing it, and as I was quoted in a recent interview, my career is thankfully not a quick snapshot. The photograph of my career at age thirty-five is more like a Polaroid picture. It is still developing, and so am I.

Waking up early is sometimes a result of a good adrenaline flow. I could not seem to shut it off. The Tigers were in town before we hit the road again to Philly and St. Louis. Obviously, my blood boiled a bit, pitching against a former team where some ill will heightened my drive. Not only did my day start well, catching up with father-and-son time, but I'd had enough time do a drive-thru with teammate Clint Barmes at our local spot, BeanThru. Caffeine had become a must, as a vitamin to keep us up as our bodies talked loudly. Anything to get through another game, and anything to trick our bodies into following suit with what our minds spoke. Not to mention, it tricked us into playing like it could be our last when in reality, a half of a season was left. The BeanThru and their coffee became such a regular staple that one of my tweets still makes its home on their website. "Jason Grilli...a BeanThru regular!"

The feeling that it would be a great day continued as I got to the field and learned that our custom-tailored suits were in. All the guys who ordered them were trying on their suits, and I could not help but laugh as we looked like we were getting ready for a road trip, but in our younger brother's closet. The suits were either mismeasured, or the style did not fit the athletes' bodies. I could not help but laugh at the stitching of the suits as each thread hung on for dear life. The poor saleswoman was in panic mode, but this was an extension of good clubhouse fun playing out. It was a riot, watching everyone looking around as if a good prank was being played on us.

Arriving at the yard is always fun, especially when you see some type of package that you may or not be expecting. This time, a few sheets of paper grabbed my attention. It was the player ballot for All-Star voting. Unlike many times before, my name was actually on the ballot for that year's mid-summer classic. For the first time, my name would not have to be written in to get a vote. Trying to recall the many times that I wished my name was on the ballot, my day of wishing and wanting had arrived. I was ecstatic inside, and my adrenaline spiked without taking a 5-hour Energy drink. I would have to come back later to vote for whomever I believed deserved to make the team and to contemplate some difficult decisions.

Trying to get in my routine after several welcomed interruptions, like the one provided by Astor and Black, I was able to put some closure on the issues I had with sports radio station 93.7 The Fan. When a shock jock couldn't think of anything else to discuss, he tossed a wild steroid allegation in my direction. The head manager came in to apologize to me directly, and he told me the situation was being handled with disciplinary action. I was appreciative of the gesture, but I still wanted to express the severity of the problem their sports shock jock could have potentially caused for me. Piggybacking on the Clemens case, I did not want my name or my reputation to be lumped in with him that way. After living through the steroid era, it felt like I received a slap in the face following the hard work I put into recovery to get where I am now.

The All-Star ballot was sitting in my locker, and it was time to vote. I discussed with a teammate who we thought was worthy, and we went over some easy, clear-cut choices. I was not sure if he had planned to put a check next to my name, or if he really felt that I was worthy, but nonetheless, I got a teammate vote. I was not sure if voting for myself felt right, but I badly wanted to go play at Kauffman Stadium, and it was not the time to hold back and be humble. I was having a good first half and felt worthy enough to check the box next to my own name, despite not being a closer. No one understood more than me what it took to get there. It was not time spent sitting in a deer stand or with a fishing pole, waiting for it to happen. It was waking up to monstrous training sessions, and I looked forward to them ending. It was rehab sessions that made me see Lucky Charms in front of my face. It was the BST (blood, sweat, and tears) that consumed me, and it was the motivation to save my family from financial ruin.

I prepared, as I always did, to get ready to pitch against the Tigers. The game played out as I had hoped, and A.J. Burnett did a fine job, posting a quality start and turning it over to our nasty bullpen. The heart of the order was due up, and I was to face Quintin Berry, Miguel Cabrera, and Prince Fielder. No short order. My mind was clear, and I was pumped up. I said to myself, "If you want this All-Star vote, go get it. This 1-2-3-punch will look like puppy chow, compared to the lineup you'll be facing on July 10th." I was locked in for a good 1-2-3 inning and threw eleven out of twelve for strikes to retire the side and rack up another hold. I got Berry on strikes and the other two big guys on weak grounders, before turning it over to our closer, Hanny, who took care of the rest to take game one of the series.

I got an extra ballot and put it in my bag to take home. I could not wait to share it with everyone. To be considered great and get some long-awaited recognition was all I ever wanted out of this game. I was bursting with pride, and my spirit was overjoyed. Even if I didn't make the All-Star game, in my mind, I'd already won. To just be considered is hard in this game, a home of so many talented and respectable players—players who I wanted to be like and be considered to be on their level of talent.

It was amazing to think when I was on the dirt bump 60' 6" away from home plate that all my boyhood dreams had finally come true. Though as a child, it was nothing but a longshot and a fantasy like every little boy dreams of, but I now found myself on par with the best players in the world. I live each day putting on a uniform that makes me feel like a superhero. All the chaos and distractions of the world around me seemed to come into focus as I left the bullpen, and the quietest place on Earth was the ballpark as I slipped my foot into that dug-out hole in front of the rubber. Roberto Clemente was right. There is a sign with his quote when I go down the tunnel that reads, "When I put on my uniform, I feel I am the proudest man on earth." I could not agree more.

Early morning wake-up calls were no longer required. I usually woke either to take out the dog, or from my own built-in Google alert since my adrenaline was pumping. I also tried to enjoy brief moments while my family slept next to me, and I savored the quiet moments while they slept. After the day's game, I'd be back on the road again. Jayse was at the impressionable age of four, where he did not want Dad to leave and couldn't wait until I came back. I cried inside, trying to be tough as I pushed forward to make the year a significant period in my career. I relished the thought and considered what I would do if I were announced to the All-Star team. The whole reason I worked so hard was to get back home, so that Jayse could enjoy sharing the game with Daddy. The envy I have always had of the picture when dads and their sons got to watch blasts during the homerun derby was within my grasp. Another tear ran down my cheek. I grew emotional thinking those thoughts that were pinned on a corkboard somewhere in my head, as they were now so close to being a reality.

Good friend and former NFL wide receiver for the Kansas City Chiefs, Eddie Kennison, called me one day while I was in the middle of a rehab session. He told me of the dream he had one night that I was going to be playing in Kansas City in the All-Star game. Well, his dream was now a possible reality. Whether it was words of encouragement or something he truly saw in me, it meant a lot to have someone believe in that wild goal of mine. His sharing of positive energy helped me get through what could have been another challenging day.

A fair amount of Detroit fans wouldn't agree. I was the brunt of a lot of boos at Comerica Park, house of the Tigers. That is what motivated me to pitch well against my former team. As a Tiger, the fans literally booed me out of town. My ERA on the road was under 2.00, but at home, it was north of 5.00. So overall, my ERA was hovering in the low 3s. Every appearance at home brought out the boo-birds. It got tougher and tougher to pitch there. It's not easy being booed by your hometown fans.

During interleague play, I got to redeem myself against my former team while wearing a Pirate uniform. I relieved twice during that series and I have to admit, I was out for blood. The first night I faced them, I had clean innings. My second appearance included 2 Ks in an inning's work and boy, what a feeling. It gave me a bit of vindication just knowing that the boo-birds were eating a bit of crow.

Clint approached me at dinner in the Pirate Cafe and asked me if I thought that I closed the book on the Tigers and buried that in my past. I said, "Yes, Skip. Absolutely, or at least until the next time I have to face them."

We ended the series with a 3-2 loss to the Tigers, as Verlander shut us down, dropping our record to 38-33 as we headed to Philadelphia to play the Phillies and to St. Louis to take on the Cards to end June. We would have loved to be in the forties on the plus side as we entered July.

Citizens Bank Park in Philly can be an intimidating place to play, although The Super Phillies were no more. Their lineup was filled with a lot of drama and players who seemed to be tired of their amazing streak of greatness. Just the same, a lineup with Rollins, Ruiz, Pence, and Victorino isn't one to sneeze at. The best part of my day was when I was doing my pre-game work, and the Phillies' bullpen catcher told me he thought Philadelphia had made a mistake letting me go, especially upon seeing what I had been able to accomplish. I had a lump in my throat thinking about that, and I couldn't have had a better moment to quietly reflect. I looked back, and I was grateful to the Phillies for helping me jumpstart my career, but I couldn't help but wonder how they failed to see what I could have contributed to their roster. I understand that scouting is not a perfect science, and mistakes can be made, but what kind of report allows you to mistake a Triple-A also-ran with an All-Star-candidate reliever? That would be sort of like the Pujols' scouting report saying that he has warning track power but will never hit in Big League ballparks. The Phillies had signed me as a major-league insurance policy, and they never had any sincere interest in making me part of their Big League plan unless someone went down. Sheff actually felt that the Phillies had just signed Halladay, Cliff Lee, and Roy Oswalt and became a little bit arrogant. Sheff had told me, "Mark my words: they're going to fail. Any time you win the World Series on paper and think you don't have to play a game, you are destined to fail." Sure enough, once again, the man in my corner was right.

After two nights off, I finally got to pitch in a barn-burner game, and it felt like forever since I'd trotted out of the bullpen door. It was time to shove it to Ruben and company and to remind them they messed up again. I am sure my age and injury-prone label would have been their excuse as to why they did not want to give me a chance at their bullpen. Yet my 0.83 ERA while a proud member of their Lehigh Valley IronPigs should have been good enough to take a shot.

Fans were rowdy, and this adrenaline junky caught a rush at an opportune time. I couldn't wait to get into the ballgame and had a rocking chair 1-2-3 inning, thanks in large part to Cutch making an unreal catch in the right centerfield gap. Off the bat, there were 30,000 fans who didn't think he'd get to it—and two who knew he would, me and Cutch. He sprawled out like Superman and made the grab. They say you need to have strength up the middle to win, and with that dude patrolling centerfield, winning was starting to become a habit.

We ended up with forty wins in our first seventy-five and headed to St. Louis to close out June with three. St. Louis has become my "rejuvenation station." There was not much to do there aside from see the Arch from our hotel room and go play ball. This time through, it was appropriate to do nothing. The temperatures were sweltering, reaching 108. We played our balls off there and also mixed in a few laughs by taking pitchers, Jared Hughes and Eric Fryer, to see the movie *Ted*. It was great to have a few laughs to break up the mundane routine that can occur during each trip through.

I did not pitch there, but it was okay, because I had plenty of time to contribute to stressful situations. Taking two out of three from the Cardinals was great, and that put us at a high-water mark to date with seven games over .500. The strong current was still flowing as the team continued to shape itself around all we were accomplishing. The Pirates were no surprise anymore. I was hopeful that they could trade for that big stick to back up McCutchen who was having an MVP season.

I experienced a tough pill to swallow before we left for the Burgh again. Before leaving on Sunday at noon we had a team meeting, and they announced the All-Star selections for the year. My name was not called. I was disappointed and felt snubbed and slighted, but I acknowledge the fact that there are only so many spots and a lot of guys feel they've earned the right to play. Typically, setup guys don't get recognition, but Mike Sweeney spoke glowingly about me on MLB Network, and that provided me some validation that I wasn't too far off with my self-evaluation. It goes to show you that the politics of baseball exist. I guess the anticipation of it all and the edge it gave me to continue to prove people wrong would get me to the place where a contract extension or multi-year deal would be a reality.

All in all, it was bullshit, and I was pissed more than I thought I would be. I'd get some time to chill at home, which was likely just as necessary. It would have been nice to be in the game the first year I was on the ballot, and missing out on my favorite stadium in the league was not easy to stomach, but it sure was motivation to catapult me into the next year.

CHAPTER 16

THE FANS OF PITTSBURGH DESERVED BETTER

> *"Why does everyone talk about the past? All that counts is tomorrow's game."*
> *~ Roberto Clemente*

Fireworks were in the air as our team heated up, and Sutton hit a walk-off round-tripper after a few comebacks. This showed the resilience and development of a Cinderella story happening in Pittsburgh. We were eight games over .500 for the first time since the 1992 team led by none other than infamous Barry Bonds. The Pirates won the division with a record of 96-66 for their third division title in a row. Those were the good ol' days in the Burgh, and those are the days that our fans were hungry to see return.

That night, Burnett threw five innings and gave up six runs. Resop, Cruz, and I held it down after taking the lead in the eighth. As pissed as I still was about my All-Star snubbing, the only ones who'd pay for it were opposing batters, not my teammates. I might not have been fun to be around for a while, but I continued to do my job every day I was called upon to do it. I punched two tickets to get to 50 Ks at the midway point. Hanny came in and was within one strike of getting another save. The Astros tied it up, and then we got one last at bat. Drew Sutton drove a breaking pitch to dead center to win the ballgame. It was a great moment for him and a great moment for our club to continue the good vibes we'd been riding. We were once again sharing first place with the Reds. I was hopeful that our GM could pull off the mother trade that would help us stay way out in front to contend, to get Pittsburgh back into the winning column, and to end the drought of nineteen seasons. We were taking care of business on the field, and there was no telling what scenarios were being drawn up in the front office as the trade deadline approached.

After sweeping four from the Astros and two of three from the Giants pre-break, all but Hanrahan and McCutchen enjoyed three days off for the break. Still, I'd have liked to join them, but the three days at home was nice and much needed.

After a bittersweet All-Star break, it was great to get back to the daily grind. It's amazing how a few days off can give you a different perspective. My baseball leather couch hugged me as I was leaving, as if to say, "Don't get hurt," and "I will be waiting for you when you return."

We opened the second half in Milwaukee, and I was greeted with the middle of the order. I faced Ryan Braun as my first hitter and walked him before getting Ramirez to fly out, and then I gave up a bloop single to Corey Hart. My arm was achy as if to say, "Why do you want me to do this again?" It was fun, as always, to be back in a city that agrees with me and the meaningful and meaningless memories I had made there.

I'd traveled from Milwaukee to Colorado, and the past few days there in Denver were a bit tough as all the distractions caught up with me. After getting back from the All-Star break, I felt a little out of sorts, but this was more because of a personal issue than wallowing in self-pity about missing the game. When you are about to get on a plane and head in the opposite direction, you question what you are doing in life and what really matters. My world turned a bit upside down and it reminded me that I am not in control of everything. I was always tested and forever will be. This was a tough feeling to shake, and I would be lying to say that I was not preoccupied with life at home. My quiet place on the mound was a bit distracted and my performance in Colorado was below par because of it. That's what fans sometimes don't realize. Only if we are machines can we go out day in and day out and not let things outside of the mound affect our performance. That's why those who can block out things and focus on the mound tend to be elite performers.

I lost the game for us after Pedro Álvarez tied up the game with a three-run shot in the top of the ninth. I unraveled and killed a comeback rally with two singles and a sac fly. It was a horrible feeling to lose another game. It was a slow death because I had been so dominant, and if I lost a game, it was normally just on one pitch that left the yard.

Even in our win two days later, I made things interesting as I walked Cuddyer, got Fowler to pop up a bunt, and then gave up a hit to Scutaro before being pulled. Watson came in to pick me up and held onto the win.

Texas is not my favorite place, let alone Houston. For some reason, I didn't enjoy going there all that much, maybe because it was a place that brought back a painful memory: when I was notified that I had been released of duties from them. I remember the feeling of helplessness and was at a low point, feeling disowned by a team I'd been so excited to be a part of. I gathered my belongings, not knowing which direction to turn.

While in Houston, there was also a sense of cabin fever because it was usually so hot I didn't want to go outside. The walk from the hotel to the bus was the only time I journeyed outside before heading into Minute Maid Park, which has a retractable dome. Sitting in the bullpen gets to be a bit much too, battling the mosquitos and feeling like a caged animal. I couldn't wait to get into the game and release the rage, or maybe that was just another cup of coffee coming into play.

We'd been playing well and needed to continue to do so in the series against the Astros. They were the team we needed to beat to keep pace with the Reds and to have momentum during our big road trip. Wandy Rodríguez, our newest addition, was facing his former team and he kept things even as Resop got the win, Lincoln got the hold, and I got the save. It was my second of the season and fifth overall in my career. We were sitting at 58-42 after 100 games, better than many of the pundits' early-season predictions. Finally, it felt great to throw through another dead spot and the physical feeling everyone has at that point in the year. The dog days were creeping in, but it was a great feeling that night to get the save.

The band MercyMe was playing live on the field, and their song was an appropriate message to help me cope with the inner battles that we all have. It was great to catch up with Bart and Robbie of the band afterward, too. There were signs all over the place that echoed my comeback loud and clear. Even while looking at the sink while brushing my teeth, I noticed a shamrock carved into the drain. It said *McGuire* on it.

I write "CG" for my grandmother, Catherine McGuire Giampietro, in the dirt as a dedication to a woman so dear to my heart, and it felt like a sign that she was right with me in that very moment.

All things were good at that moment. We had a chance to do something great and make history. All signs pointed to a good shot in Pittsburgh through our 100th game. I hoped we could finish what we started and reward the city of Pittsburgh for their two decades of suffering while continuing to stand by us.

I pitched another solid inning against the Cubs to start August, racking up another 2 Ks. I love punching tickets more than anything. There was no better feeling of dominance than sitting a guy down on the pine and watching him scratch his head as he hopes he doesn't have to face you next time around.

With the trade deadline looming, I was glad to have arrived at the clubhouse late for this series, because I knew the guys who were coming and going in the tiny Wrigley Field clubhouse were going to be in an uncomfortable situation. My gut instincts were right, because when I arrived, I spoke with McCutchen who told me that McGehee got traded to the Yankees and found out via television. This just goes to show that we are not in control and that this is a business and not always a game. I love the game, hate the business.

With the trade deadline behind us, we headed to New York with most of the same faces. Funny how I could sit in the quiet confines of my hotel room and be at peace while being twenty-four floors above an electric city like Manhattan. Maybe it was because I thought of being there in my home state, albeit three hours away from home. Or maybe it was because I attended college there that made it seem ironic that the season-ending grind was celebrated in the silence of my swanky room on Park Avenue at the Grand Hyatt.

I'd been through a ton to get to that point, and with only nine games to go to end the season, I focused on me instead of the team for a change. I wanted to get into at least three more games in order to reach a bonus incentive of $50,000 for appearances and to end on a high note as I began off-season negotiations.

Going to Citi Field and checking it off my bucket list of stadiums in which I'd pitched left me with only one to appear in (Target Field in Minnesota). It felt good to go early and look around a beautiful ballpark nestled in the crisp fall New York air. I felt like I was home, and it was nice to reminisce and feel comforted after what I'd become over the course of the long season. My intense nature and desire to fight was caught up in the reflection of what I had accomplished to get there. More so than ever, I relished the joy of being in a place that felt familiar, a place where I belonged, while feeling a sense of satisfaction that I accomplished what I'd set out to do.

During batting practice while a handful of my teammates shagged flies, I actually had to fight back tears. I allowed a lot to filter through my mind while I stood in the outfield. As fly balls buzzed all around me and my teammates chased them down, I stood in a temporary daydream, thinking how much of life had passed me by while I tried to chase this dream. I had a moment of reflection as I thought about the family I hardly ever saw and how out of touch I was with so many who loved and supported me. It is the reality many don't understand unless they experience it themselves. As awesome as this life seems to be, there are downsides that are never considered by those who haven't played the game. As Atticus Finch said in *To Kill a Mockingbird*, "You never really understand a person until you consider things from his point of view...Until you climb into his skin and walk around in it."

It was a shame that many of my teammates were frustrated beyond belief about the collapse of our season. It had been a total disappointment as we tried collectively to change history and give Pittsburgh a winning team. There were a lot of excuses as to why we failed, but mostly there were reasons.

I have my opinions on why and how, but the way we performed

was the main cause. However, I like to think positively, and I felt that forgetting each event would keep my thoughts optimistic and focused on what I needed to do next season to get the team over the hump. Otherwise, I'd be elsewhere doing the same for another team.

I was interested to see what would be discussed in my exit meeting with the staff and front office. This was something that was done the year prior, when we were in Los Angeles. Hurdle, Huntington, pitching Coach Ray Searage, and bullpen coach Euclides Rojas were all in the meeting to share their observations with me and about me as a person and a player.

It looked as if each of us would be celebrating individual accomplishments instead of celebrating our first winning season in twenty years. We gave it a good 120 games, but unfortunately the 2012 season went down the same way as the nineteen seasons before it—with a losing record.

Everyone was both mentally and physically fatigued, so I decided to stay in my hotel room and reflect on my past seasons. I persevered through adversity. I had a life decision to make to drag my family overseas. I stuck it out. A year earlier, I chose pride over money and the offer to play in Korea. I believed in myself and fought through all the injuries, the steroid decision, and whether or not to join the majority. I shook off the labels placed on me and proved my abilities to get to this point in my career. It felt so sweet, and I basked in the joy of what I'd accomplished with support of my family.

CHAPTER 17

THERE'S NO PLACE LIKE HOME

///

> *"Guys ask me, don't I get burned out? How can you get burned out doing something you love? I ask you, have you ever got tired of kissing a pretty girl?"*
>
> ~ Tommy Lasorda

November was upon us. The free agent season had officially opened, and I felt like the kid in *The Bad News Bears*. You'll remember the pitcher at the end who played for the Yankees, who holds the ball just to spite his dad. I felt that after all the hard work I put myself through, I finally got to hold the ball and enjoy the control I had. I relished it. Even Sheff enjoyed negotiating for me because for once, I was in the position of power.

With my future and the future of my family on the line, I came through like I always knew I was capable of doing. One of two things could have happened: I'd come into the season with the metaphorical bases loaded, no one out, and I could have either crapped my drawers in front of millions of fans or I could have punched out the side to win the game. When the season ended, my shorts were clean and there were three opposing players headed to the dugout dragging their bats behind them.

Many believed I was about to hit the lottery. That was not what I was playing for or ever have played for. Sure, the money part was what I prayed for repeatedly while lying on my bunk in my faux Hall of Fame as a kid. All my heroes surrounded me in the form of posters that adorned my bedroom walls, and I'd look up to them as if they were real, trying to absorb their powers and learn from the lessons they had learned while playing the game. It was a visionary thing. I had the vision and the determination to succeed.

Then reality would hit. I had an alarm clock waking me up at 6:00 AM in the snowy town of Syracuse, only to hear my teachers telling me to keep studying. "That is a lofty dream," they'd say. "Now get real, and get back to studying."

I told Mrs. Goff, "I will make it, and I will come back and sign your chalkboard one day." I did, and she cried after hugging me and apologizing, saying, "I'm sorry. I didn't know you were that good." I thanked her for motivating me and for being a great teacher. I earned an A in her class to prove that my studies were important, too.

Can't has been a motivating word for me. I somehow thought things would be easier being a first-round pick, thinking I was immune to injury. Yet there I was, fifteen years later, waiting for my big payday. I was working all the time, surviving all the shit just to prove to myself and to others that this was what hard work could do. I would never shoot down a kid's dreams, but I will tell him that if he really wants it, he will need to make some serious sacrifices to get it. Nothing in life is handed to you. It is all the result of hard work, perseverance, and determination.

I couldn't wait to see where I fit on the graph of free-agent signings, and I assumed I would fall somewhere between the dollar amount that Brandon League signed for (four years, $22.5 million) and Jhonny Peralta (two years, $6 million), despite the fact that I had better numbers than both of them. We'd soon see what the market warranted a guy about to turn thirty-six who was pitching like he's twenty again. It was my turn to enjoy that time and not make the same mistakes I'd made as a kid. The contract I'd worked for was there, and I hoped I could ride off into the sunset as I'd dreamt about many years ago.

Though there could be other places willing to pay me more, my goal was to re-sign with the Pirates. I believed we had the foundation in place to take it to the next level in 2013, and I wanted to be in the right place at the right time instead of leaving one season before the flower bloomed. Pittsburgh gave me my shot, and Gary and I discussed this at length after the season ended. The Pirates were the team that gave me my opportunity. "Anytime a team gives you an opportunity when no one else did," explained Sheff, "we honor that. If you honor that, it is going to honor you."

Our plan was to entertain offers and see what was out there. Obviously, if someone overwhelmed us with an offer that was bigger and better than we conceived, we would, of course, consider it, but our goal was to return to Pittsburgh. It's close to home, my family enjoyed the city, and I expected big things from the Pirates in the upcoming season.

I remembered having a conversation with my dad when I was a kid about my dream to be a number-one pick. He always encouraged me and thought it was a great goal, but an awfully daunting task with a high degree of improbability. He didn't shoot down my dream, but I knew that in his heart of hearts, he couldn't comprehend that his son was going to be a top pick, and if he did, he had a lot to prove and a lot of work to do to make it happen.

Even my high school teachers snickered and stated that was a great goal, but to be sure to continue my studies, because school was more important and a necessary fallback in case my pie-in-the-sky goal didn't materialize.

I loved the library and my studies were always important to me, top-round pick or not, but my heart was always on the ball field. Some days, if we had library time to work on group projects, I would wish I could sneak away and leave the class project behind. In my mind, I always thought I had a good reason.

There were a few windows facing our high school baseball field, and when I'd sit and try to study, the mound was in clear sight, calling my name much louder than the class project. I always carried a ball instead of an apple in my backpack, and it would come out during those indiscrete moments. I was a good student, so I felt that any time I fell into a daydream about becoming a Big Leaguer, I allowed it. My teachers would bring me back to reality when they noticed I had drifted away, and they'd tell me to focus on my group project and the part of school that was likely more of a reality.

Sometimes you just know things, though, and trying to explain this to my family and my teachers was futile. They thought they knew how things were going to turn out, but they had absolutely no idea! I was out to prove everyone wrong, and I wanted it so badly. I knew I had some talent and was gifted. I think any MLB player would admit that. There are outliers in the sport who know that bigger things are to come, because they are the ones making and creating the success stories and are on the covers of their own local sports pages.

CHAPTER 18

THE MAGIC SEASON ABOARD THE JOLLY ROGER

"And they'll watch the game and it'll be as if they dipped themselves in magic waters. The memories will be so thick they'll have to brush them away from their faces."

~ Terence Mann in Field of Dreams

On the next to last day of 2012, my friend and then-Pirates closer Joel Hanrahan was traded to the Red Sox in a six-player deal. Despite saving seventy-six games in eighty-four tries over the past two seasons, Hanny knew the writing was on the wall, and such is life in a small market. When the price tag gets too high for a small market team to justify, they cash in their chips and try to get three less-expensive chips in return. I greeted the news with mixed emotions, as I was saying goodbye to a good friend and teammate, but it also opened the door for me to become the next closer for the Pittsburgh Pirates. I took a deep breath, knowing the opportunity I had discussed with Clint in shallow right field several seasons ago in Colorado was now mine to win. The Hanrahan trade also netted us Mark Melancon, who would prove to become a key ingredient to the bullpen in 2013, and who would later hatch the Shark Tank, which became the pen's identity as the season progressed.

It was exciting to get to this point but at the same time, it was a little nerve-racking when faced with the reality that it was now finally mine. I needed to be sure I didn't screw it up. I relished the opportunity and couldn't wait until spring training actually started, so I could show people that hard work pays off and if you believe in something and work your balls off, your efforts are often rewarded.

I spoke to Hanny after hearing of the trade, and he wished me luck. He knew the trade was likely to happen, because he was arbitration eligible and was going to demand twice what he was making before—a number he had rightfully earned. Since the Pirates were not going to pay him the $7 million for which he'd ultimately signed, he knew his days as a Pirate were numbered.

I think the Pirates saw my strikeout totals and what I did as a set-up man since joining the team, and they knew they could save some payroll without losing anything in regard to productivity. About 98 percent of the time, the eighth-inning guys face the heart of the order, and based on my track record, it was clear that I had few problems with those guys, so it would make sense that I could handle numbers six, seven, and eight to close out games.

During the winter and early spring, when it was clear that the closer role was mine to lose, I daydreamed about—of all things— what my closer music would be as I entered the game. Here's the big bad closer coming in, and the entrance music sets the stage. It's something I'd never had to think about, but now I had to make this critical decision. Mariano, of course, has the best entrance ever, and he should, because he is the greatest ever. Hanrahan teased me upon learning that I would be trying to fill his cleats following his departure. "Well, you'll get to pick your Pearl Jam song," he said, because he knew my song would be something from the catalog of

Eddie Vedder and the band, and he was right. I picked "Whipping." The first verse spoke directly to my career path and struck the core of what I'd gone through.

In spring training, I wanted to see my video, which would accompany the song as I exited the pen and headed to the mound before each appearance during the season. Once the season started, it would be hard not to look over my shoulder and watch the video as I ran in, so I thought I had better see it backstage, before the season started.

Opening Day arrived, and my first appearance against the Cubs was special. This one was like, "I am the closer, and I can do this." My whole family was present, as they not only knew what I had been through to get to that point, but unfortunately, they had to go through much of it with me. In many ways, reaching that moment was a testament not only to my hard work and dedication, but to that of my family, too. There was only room for one of us out on the hill, but I knew the entire Grilli family was out there with me. It was time to show up all those people who doubted me, who labeled me wrong, who thought I couldn't do this. It was time to say, "F you. Here I am."

My dad told me it was a dream of his to close. He spent his career as a middle reliever, but it's every guy's dream to be the last guy holding the ball to end the game. In all sports, people dream of catching the winning touchdown or scoring the game-winning hoop as time ticks off the clock. For a pitcher—especially a relief pitcher—the dream is to punch-out the final batter to end a game. It's a glorious thing.

At the same time, it can be tension-filled, if you let it be, or if you say to yourself, "Hey, I don't want to screw this up." If you take that approach, you're not pitching with confidence. That's a lot of pressure to have hanging over your head, knowing that in one pitch, you can screw up what your team worked eight innings to secure. That's the reason why many guys don't have it in their genetic make-up to close. It's too much pressure for some guys to handle. For me, the pressure to be able to walk again and to provide for my family was real pressure. Compared to that, taking the ball with 50,000 screaming fans and twenty-five teammates counting on you is no pressure at all.

As it turned out, we won our first game against the Cubs 3-0, with me recording the last three outs of the game, two of them being punch-outs. As Schierholtz swung and missed on a four-seamer and fireworks went off on a cold April night, I recorded my first save as an official closer. Martin rushed out to me, and I gave him a couple of shots in the chest protector as he handed me the game ball. It had been three years and a lot of PT sessions since my knee exploded, and I was now the closer of the Pittsburgh Pirates. Raise the Jolly Roger for what would be the first of many times that season.

Aside from that shakeup at the end of the pen, I think we knew, down to the man, what we had going into 2013. Maybe we didn't know how good we would be, but we certainly had an inkling that we were good. This was a huge factor in my decision to re-sign with the team, despite the fact that they did not offer me the most money. All I've ever wanted in my career was to have an opportunity to show what I could do and to be in the midst of a championship team, and it seemed evident that I was going to get both opportunities if I stayed a part of the 2013 Pittsburgh Pirates.

I knew the level of talent that was there and saw the progress that the organization had made since I arrived in 2011. There was a feeling in the town and with this group of guys that hadn't been felt since before many of these players were born. The team was made up of scrappy, hard-nose ballplayers who hadn't yet hit their prime, and I wanted to be a part of it. I have said throughout my career that

I was always at the right place at the wrong time. It seemed as though I was a day late and a dollar short, as the Marlins, Rockies, Rangers, and Indians all reached the playoffs after I left. I wasn't going to let this one pass me by, and I made damn sure I put my signature on the dotted line to be a part of their team. Sometimes you can bet red all day long, but every once in a while, black is going to hit, too. Whether we were a World Series-caliber team or not, who could be sure? But I knew that we were playoff bound, and once you get to the dance, anything can happen.

I had a strong conviction that this team was the real deal for two reasons. I felt we could win there in Pittsburgh, based on the players that we had and the pieces they kept adding, and from a selfish point, I knew how much I could help the ball club, from not only a performance standpoint, but also from a leadership standpoint. Though I have shied away from being a soapbox kind of guy, I believe the key to being a strong leader is to keep the guys loose and having fun, and I believe that we'd developed that type of *esprit de corps* over the past several seasons. The seeds had been planted; it was time to germinate, bloom, and blossom.

Following our limp to the finish line in 2011 and 2012, I think the team learned that we needed to lose a little bit to appreciate winning. Just as Team Italy had to go through a maturation process from year to year where they went from just happy to be there to winning a game to winning a major game on the big stage to advancing to the second round, we, too, were in the process of advancing based on our past losses. It was rare that a team steps into the box and wins a World Championship, especially a young team. It took baby steps to get to the dance, and each time we got in the ring and took a few hits, we got stronger, tougher, and more seasoned. We may not have won in 2011 or 2012, but we took our lumps and grew stronger from the experience. I believed in my heart that we were ready to take yet another step in 2013. Whether it would be the big step or not was left to be seen, but I was confident we would be a contender.

Prior to 2013, we were missing a few pieces to take us to the next level, and that spoke to experience as much as it did to talent. They started building several years before to create a strong core with high-round draft picks, good players, young players, and talented players. Then they sprinkled in some experienced players, and the core kept getting bigger. It is kind of like a snowball turning into an avalanche.

One offseason addition that really paid dividends was the signing of free agent catcher Russell Martin who'd last played for the Yankees. The Yankees let him walk, and they struggled with their catching all season while we signed Russell for two years and $17 million and got a quality receiver. I had heard he was good, but I didn't realize just how important he was to the staff until I had the opportunity to work with him. Prior to his arrival, teams were running all over us, so having a guy who could help pitchers as a quality receiver while also keeping runners at bay was a luxury we didn't previously have. If you add what he ended up doing for us offensively, especially considering how much he played, his meaning to the team couldn't be quantified. Plus, he had experience as a winner, and that was the type of intangible that makes all the difference in the world.

If the team had one superstar amongst the cast of twenty-five members, it was without a doubt Andrew McCutchen. Since the Pirates have had several low finishing season standings, the organization has had the opportunity to pick high in the draft, McCutchen being one of them. He doesn't say a lot in the clubhouse, but he speaks up when he needs to. He is the consummate definition of *lead by example*, because when guys see how good he is and how hard he plays, it automatically causes them to elevate their game. There was one game in San Diego where he hit a ball to the opposite field on a 3-0 pitch, and I said to the rest of the bullpen, "That is the kind of stuff that earns you the MVP." He is so good and without him, we wouldn't be anywhere near the team that we are. Players see how hard he runs out a ground ball, even when he knows he's going to be out on a double play, and how his feet barely touch the ground when he goes from first to third, and it is clear that this guy expects to win every time he puts on the uniform. He's so fast that many plays he makes don't make the SportsCenter reel, because he makes them look so easy, while other guys screw up a fly ball so badly that they make the routine plays look like highlights. He's shown that he's earned his current contract, but when he's up for his next contract, it will be hard for a small-market team like ours to keep him. Lord knows, we should enjoy every moment while he's wearing the black and gold.

From the start of spring training, I thought the bullpen had the chance to be dominant. I knew we had talent, power arms, and guys with great stuff, but I wasn't sure how good we would be. We were young, and sometimes that naiveté can be a plus, and the best thing was we were each put into positions where we could be successful. We could see what type of ball club we could have in the first month of the season, and I think one of our strong suits was our bullpen. We were able to keep one and two-run games close, and we formed an incredibly tight unit down there. If you look at our numbers for the season, we were arguably the best bullpen in the league, and some of us older guys did some things to create an identity. The guys kept talking about what they were going to name themselves. I chuckled and explained that it can't be some sort of self-proclaimed name. It has to be something that evolves and takes on an existence of its own. You can't create your own moniker, as it could almost become folly. As the world now knows, we became known as the Shark Tank, courtesy of our token underwater adventurer, Mark Melancon.

As the pen began to jell and take on an identity, people kept asking what we were going to call ourselves. Melancon was a Twitter newbie and came to me to find out the ins and outs on how to use the social media network. It's no secret that I am known as the resident social media guru, so he and I were talking about it in the pen during a game. He shared a story that during the offseason, he was out in New Zealand being an ambassador for baseball. During an off day, he and his wife decided to go scuba diving, and they went swimming with the sharks. The two of them were immersed in the water in a steel cage and not only swam with the sharks, but he had one named after him. Somewhere in the deep waters off the coast of New Zealand swims a shark named Melancon. So, once he became versed in the ways of Twitter, the first picture he posted up there was his namesake from down under, Melancon.

In my role as one of the elder statesmen of the pen, I encouraged the younger guys to demand excellence from themselves, to be aggressive, and each time they take the ball, they should expect at least one punch-out from themselves. So, after a while, instead of using the phrase "punch his ticket" to represent a strikeout victim, we started using the phrase, "He's going to get bit." High-fives were soon replaced by a hand gesture that resembled a shark's fin and aptly named "high-fins." I took the evolution of the Shark Tank a step further and researched whether or not there was a pet shark we could adopt without having to purchase a five-hundred-gallon tank. Finally, after a few conversations, I found Gary Knabe at Elmer's Aquarium in Monroeville, who was generous enough to donate a 150-gallon fish tank, two sand sharks, a grouper, and a puffer fish. I told him who I was and asked if we could work out a barter-type deal where he'd donate and maintain the tank, and in turn, he was rewarded with endless publicity, local news stories, tweets, and even a mention in *Sports Illustrated*.

The Shark Tank name became public during an interview with ESPN radio. The interviewer said, "You know you guys are so good, what do you attribute it to?" I told him we're like a bunch of sharks down there. We're hungry, and anytime we get on the mound, we smell blood, and we start a frenzy and go for the kill. We just attack. Well, the moment that got out on the airwaves, the name spread like wildfire, and we were officially deemed the "Shark Tank."

We named one of the sharks Teke after the greatest Pirates closer of all time, Kent Tekulve, who pitched in over 1,000 games over sixteen seasons. The other one was unofficially named Cutter, though he didn't quite get the press and the glory that Teke did. Ironically, the only time the sharks showed any signs of life was during feeding time, when we would put some shrimp or squid in the water. The whole analogy was in perfect harmony with life in the bullpen. We sat down there quietly for six or seven innings, and as soon as soon as the bullpen phone rings, we start swimming around and go in for the proverbial kill.

Melancon came to the team as part of the trade that sent Hanrahan to the Red Sox, and though he had a challenging season with Boston in 2012, he was a perfect fit for us. He and I combined at the end of the game to form a near-untouchable combination. If a pen can shorten the game for their team, the starters know that if they get through the sixth inning with the lead, their team will usually come out with a "W."

We didn't just have one closer down there in me, we had a bunch of closers who knew their roles and knew what they needed to do to succeed. It was one guy's role to close out the sixth inning and someone else's to close out the seventh, Melancon closed the eighth, and I closed the ninth. Each of us had closer mentality, but we brought it to the hill at a different part of the game. That was why when some reporter would stick a microphone under my nose at the end of the game, I'd often point to Wilson, Watson, Mazzaro, Gomez, Hughes, Morris, and all the guys swimming around in the Shark Tank. They may not have had the ball when the final out was recorded, but they got us to that point and deserved just as much credit. "What about that guy there? He had a key moment in the fifth inning. Interview him. I came in with a clean inning and got three pressure-free outs. Go interview him." Pitching as the closer is just like running a relay race, where I happen to receive the baton last. If the legs before me don't do their job and put us in a position to win, my leg isn't likely to mean much. I just happen to be the guy who breaks the tape at the end of the race and get all the fans screaming my name. It was actually my goal that, rather than me getting forty or fifty saves, I would prefer that everyone else got at least one.

I tried to impress upon the young guys, even those guys who didn't know my story, how important and unheralded the role of the middle reliever is. It is the baseball equivalent to the offensive line in that if you are good, the quarterback gets all the headlines, and if you are bad, then people start noticing you. It is perhaps the most thankless job in sports, this side of the extra point holder and the O line in football. The middle reliever comes in with runners on first and third and one out, and he has to make a pitch. The closer oftentimes comes in with a clean inning, and the only time he gets in a mess is if he creates it himself. I served in that role, and I did a good job at it. That is what groomed me to be a closer. It is part of the process, just as learning how to win as a team is part of the process. It is a rare individual who steps into the game as a kid, is handed the ball and knows how to effectively close games over an extended period.

At the end of each win, different groups in the lineup each developed their own superstitions that became part of the team mystique. Baseball players are a very superstitious lot, and if something works for you once, you keep on going to the well. My trademark became punching Martin in the chest protector. I don't really know how it happened. I wear my heart on my sleeve, and after the first save of the season, I was so fired up that I grabbed him in a headlock (he is much shorter than I am), and I gave him a couple of chest pounds. I ended up with twenty-five straight saves to start the season, so I'll be damned if I change my routine with that type of consistency on the line. So the chest punch was born. These are the things that keep you going during the long season, and once you find something that works, it takes on a life of its own. Chemistry is often talked about in baseball. The intangibles are important in building a championship team. These little nuances build chemistry. In some ways, these are the atoms that combine to build molecules, which eventually interact to become team chemistry.

Everyone on the team got along. There was no ego and no animosity toward one another. When you are lucky enough to build a team with a bunch of guys who enjoy each other and are pulling in the same direction, and then sprinkle in a huge dose of talent, it creates a great recipe for winning. Even the late additions like Byrd, Buck, and Morneau, who management brought in to bolster our chances of going deep into the playoffs, were perfect additions to the team.

Even though we came up short, it made us wish that the same group of guys would come into camp in 2014, because we have some unfinished business left on the field. When you learn what winning tastes like, you hope they don't dismantle things and start fresh but instead build on what we'd started and keep the nucleus intact. The process they put together there worked. The players they brought in worked. We wanted them to leave it together, add a few pieces here and there, and bring home a championship to the extremely deserving city of Pittsburgh.

Pittsburgh is, without question, the City of Champions. I can't say enough about the people of Pittsburgh. Their passion for the sport and everything they gave to me since the moment I arrived proved it. The love that they give is indescribable. I have never felt that anywhere else I played, and the appreciation they have for guys who go out and play hard is a testament to the blue-collar mentality these people have had instilled in them for generations. If you lose yet play hard, they accept that. If you don't play hard, they won't stand for it. These are the salt-of-the-earth people. I love Pittsburgh because it is so not pretentious despite the fact that it is a beautiful city. As a city, their attitude is *What can I do for you?* That sentiment is absent anywhere else I've ever played.

What made playing together even more fun was how the city went absolutely nuts. The city saw something in us they hadn't seen in years here. Fans would come up to me on the street, and with tears in their eyes and cracks in their voices, they'd thank me for helping bring a passion to the team and to the city that they hadn't witnessed in a long time. We need to remember that Pittsburgh is a steel town that had been hit relatively hard by the slow economy and the loss of jobs to other countries. Like many of the industrial cities throughout the east and the Midwest, they hadn't had a lot to cheer about on a day-in and day-out basis. That is another reason that the city became so energized by our success.

Like the city, the Pirates hadn't been synonymous with winning in decades. To be able to experience the accompanying feeling of jubilation meant a lot to the psyche of my teammates and the self-esteem of the city. Fans came up to me on several occasions during the year and tearfully thanked us, saying things like, "Thank you, thank you. We're not a doormat here in Pittsburgh." I think that's why I love the city so much. It's because I could relate to what it was like to feel like a doormat, and I was grateful that the city, in turn, gave me the opportunity to prove that I wasn't.

That's what sports do for a city. They bring people together. For twenty years, those people hadn't been able to feel pride in their baseball team, and now for the first time in the lives of many of the fans, they renewed the pride of wearing the black and gold with Pirates emblazoned across their chests instead of feeling like laughingstocks. It gives you a patriotic feeling to believe in something. Fans look forward to waking up each day and grabbing the newspaper first thing to check out whether or not their team won the night before. We changed the culture of what people felt around Pittsburgh. For once, it wasn't the Steelers or the Penguins giving them something to look forward to in the fall and winter. They could look forward to spring training and summer again.

Clint and the GM came to me at our introductory meetings during spring training and told me they wanted me to create a big ripple effect. I assured them not to worry. I wore my emotions on my sleeve, and just as my father taught me to love and respect the game, I will gladly teach these guys what an honor and privilege it is to play here and that they, too, need to love and respect the game. I will create a ripple effect with my actions through example, not with jaw-flapping and motivational speeches. It was important to me to be asked because with my career heading toward an end, I wanted to instill these values in some of the younger players so they will be able to pass it on as they become the elder statesmen of their team.

At the end of May, we took three of four games from Detroit and shut down their explosive lineup in thirty-two of thirty-three innings. A lot of people asked me if I still had a vendetta against the team. I was under a lot of pressure when I pitched in Detroit, and I didn't handle it especially well, causing them to send me out of town like a half-eaten bag of chips. Now, five years later, I was pitching in a pressure role in the same city that couldn't get rid of me fast enough, and I was dominating them. It gave me a sense of gratification, but I certainly wasn't carrying out a vendetta. The highlight of the series was getting the ball in the bottom of the tenth of a 1-0 game and striking out the heart of their order: Hunter, Cabrera, and Fielder. Having the fans that booed me out of town now cheer in appreciation for what I did. The compliments you get from your peers mean more than anything, and later in the season at the July All-Star game, Miguel Cabrera came up and told me that I'm the toughest reliever he'd ever faced, while Leyland told me he was proud of me for sticking it out and flourishing. That alone was all I needed to hear to realize what a long way I had come.

About mid–June, with things clicking along pretty well for the team and me, Melancon and I were out in the pen and I said, "I got my eyes on the All-Star game. You gotta come with me." The game was in New York, which meant I could get my family there without much effort, and I wanted both me and my set-up guy to be there together. I was under consideration the year prior, but I fell short. I saw Mike Sweeney, who was working for the MLB Network out in San Diego, and he said on the air, "Grilli deserves to be there, but since he's not a closer, it's going to be tough to make it. He has closer numbers and deserves to make the All-Star team." This year, there was no reason I shouldn't make it, and I wanted to break that myth by having Melancon make it, too. To be voted in by my peers—not because I backed in or someone got injured—was really a nice feather in my cap. As I said, there is no better feeling in this game than being recognized by your peers. I was named a Futures All-Star sixteen seasons before, so whoever deemed me on their scouting report to be a future All-Star finally looked like they knew what they were talking about. What made the game even sweeter was the fact that not only did Melancon join me as an NL All-Star, but so did McCutchen, Pedro Álvarez, and Jeff Locke.

The week leading up to the All-Star game was nearly as incredible as being there. The team scheduled a father/son trip to Wrigley, and I got to room with my dad in Chicago. The team was in the locker room, which is so intimate that you're nearly rubbing cheeks with the guy next to you while dressing, and you can usually hear some guy peeing while you're eating a pre-game sandwich. Hurdle came in and announced the All-Stars. I left the locker room to see a bunch of the dads wearing their Pirates jerseys and waiting for the team to come out and stretch. I sprinted to my dad, who was in right field with McCutchen's and Charlie Morton's dads, and gave him the news. We hugged and cried together, and after texting Danielle and the rest of the family, I asked Dad if he wanted to shag some fly balls during BP. Then it was like a "field of dreams" moment when he said, "Hey, son, you wanna have a catch?" You can't script that stuff. There isn't a more special moment in a guy's life than playing catch with his father against the ivy at Wrigley on the day he makes the Major League Baseball All-Star Team.

After watching the game from home for sixteen years in a row, having my sons on my lap during the homerun derby was what it was all about. I got to do something I've always wanted to do and close that circle by including my kids in one of the greatest moments of my career. Tagg Bozied, who I'd played with at Lehigh Valley, sent me a picture of two Amish guys watching the game at a bar and said to me, "Cheese, when your kids ask you how good you were, you can show them this picture and tell them, 'I was that good, that I could make Amish guys watch me play.'"

I flew Bree, Randy, and my physical therapist, Melissa, from

Orlando. My dad referred to us as "The Avengers." That was the first time they got to meet Bree. It was pretty emotional for them to see "my angel" there with me, because they knew what a big part of my recovery she was and how important she had become to me. It was a family celebration, and it was important to me to include those people in it, who, though not blood, are as near and dear to me as a family member. Those people needed to be there, because they were so important in putting Humpty Dumpty back together again and supporting me throughout my entire recovery.

It was an incredible accomplishment to have made the team, to be there with all my family and friends, and to have experienced the home run derby with my boys. In truth, that by itself would have been enough, and if by chance I didn't make an appearance, I would have been disappointed yet still fulfilled. However, NL manager Bruce Bochy of the Giants, the team that originally drafted me, came up to me before the game began and said, "You are a great story, Jason. No matter what, you've got the ninth." I was like, "No way." To make the moment more incredible, I was essentially pitching opposite Mariano Rivera in his final All-Star appearance. "The Sandman" pitched the eighth inning for the AL and was named the deserving MVP of the game in his final season as a New York Yankee. For him, it was a momentous game. For me, not as momentous in comparison, but pretty darn big. I was able to warm up next to him in the bullpen, where he acknowledged me with a tip of the cap. These are the things you dream of.

I faced Prince Fielder, who hit a leadoff triple to start the ninth, on a ball to right field that wasn't hit very well. I made up my mind at that moment that he wasn't going to score. I didn't come all this way to give up a run in my first All-Star appearance. I had been striking out everybody left and right to get to the game, and it was kind of apropos that things started off that way for me there. In my first game in the Hawaiian League, facing my first professional hitter some sixteen years ago, I gave up a leadoff triple, too. Then I buckled down and refused to let him score. Now, nearly two decades later, I needed to duplicate that outcome. I needed to wear the cap of the middle reliever and minimize the damage, knowing that the balance of who earned the home-field advantage in the World Series rested delicately on my shoulders. I didn't want to be the guy who screwed that up for the NL and perhaps even for my own team, should we have made it. We were down 3-0 at the time, but we still hoped to rally in the ninth to win the game. A 3-0 lead was easier to overcome than anything greater. I ended up getting Cruz, Encarnacion, and Gordon on three harmless outs to leave Fielder stranded on third.

As the game ended, I was cleaning my stuff out of my locker and trying to gather my thoughts because it all went so fast. I called my dad and told him he had to come into the clubhouse and look around at the Who's Who of Baseball that had been assembled. Tony La Russa, who knew my dad from scouting with the Cardinals, walked over to us and said, "Hey, Steve, your son has one hell of a story. What a hell of a competitor. We hated when he pitched against us because we knew that it was going to be a tough inning." To hear that coming from a guy who managed a team that was in my way of getting a World Series ring was the cherry on top.

The day after the game, I ended up with my picture on the cover of *Sports Illustrated*, completing the most surreal week of my career. Dad and I went to the bank the day the issue came out, and we were practically chased down the street by about fifty fans with SI in their hands, waiting for my signature. It was cool that I got to be on the cover, but I was so glad the story was about the whole bullpen and not just about me. Without them, I wouldn't have been successful, so it was only fitting that the article was about the Shark Tank and not about me.

I ended up saving twenty-nine games prior to the All-Star game, and have to admit that each one was just as sweet as the one before. I was pitching with more confidence than I ever had. They gave me a bazooka to shoot with to make a big explosion out there. They gave me an opportunity to do my job, and I wasn't going to let it go. I really felt like I had my foot on the gas, pushed all the way to the floorboard, and I wasn't going to let up. The media was talking about me breaking Frankie Rodriguez's record for saves. Hell, I wasn't thinking about that. I was thinking about making sure I had enough left at the end of the season to make a difference when the games really mattered. My main focus is always to win. Winning the World Series matters the most.

A few days after enjoying my view from the top of the baseball world, I realized once again how fleeting that feeling of success can be. I am convinced that the heavy workload of the first half took its toll on my arm, and I suffered a tendon strain in my right arm. I was doing everything I could to stay healthy, and whether it was the infamous SI jinx or God's way of saving my bullets again, I had to shut it down for a few weeks. Thank God I took myself out when I did, because I could have hurt myself even more. It was painful, but I knew my body and I knew the injury wasn't severe. I knew something wasn't right, as my arm kept getting tighter and tighter, and it was time to pull a Roberto Durán. *No mas!*

The injury was a perfect parallel to my career path. You can find yourself at the pinnacle and then step off a curb, and in a moment, everything can be ripped away. Things can be taken from you as quickly as they are achieved, and I think it is God's way of reminding us to savor every moment and to remember who is in control.

In many ways, one of the best things that happened to the team was my injury after the All-Star game. This gave the other guys in the pen the chance to step up and fill other roles that maybe they weren't entirely comfortable with and yet they performed valiantly. So much so that it gave me extra time to heal and rest. I hated sitting on the bench after I came off the DL. I wanted to get back in there and contribute to the team, but watching how those guys performed in my absence went miles in not only allowing us to finish out the season and make the playoffs, but also continuing the maturation and the growth toward our 2014 season. Fans knew that this wasn't a flash in the pan. They knew that this team was built for the long haul and may very likely be a World Series contender for the next several seasons.

As we approached the trade deadline, we were as much in this thing as we were the previous two seasons, yet this year felt different, not only to the team, but to management. They made a conscious decision to better the team and make some additions that made us a true playoff and World Series contender by adding Marlon Byrd, John Buck, and Justin Morneau. They were a trio of solid major-league veterans who were also known as character guys. Each of them was as hungry to win a championship as the guys whom they were joining, and they were each perfect compliments to what we had there. The fact that Huntington and the front office pulled the trigger was the show of confidence we needed to continue our climb to the playoffs. I personally thanked owner Bob Nutting for being a man of his word. That bodes well with me. We were a good team without these guys. There was concern of ruining team chemistry, but those are the types of guys we needed to get us over the hump so we could have an extended life into October. We earned the attention of management and put the team in a position where they needed to make the moves to get us over the top.

As I was packing my bags at the end of the 2012 season, Nutting said to me, "Thanks for doing what you did and for being a leader. I can promise you one thing: We will do whatever it takes in the

future so that you guys and the city don't have to feel this way again."
I told him that I'm a man who's running out of time to reach my
goal of winning a ring, and I appreciated him and the team going
above and beyond to get the reinforcements to bring it home for the
city, for the team, and for me. Their actions made the whole team
feel like *This is our turn. We're going to do this.*

We clinched a playoff spot on September 23rd with a 2-1 win
against the Cubs where the tying run was gunned down at the plate,
McCutchen, to Morneau, to Martin, to win the game. The defensive
equivalent to a walk-off hit to win. That win coupled with a
Cardinals loss, and the city of Pittsburgh had a playoff team for the
first time since 1992. The irony of winning a game in this fashion
can't be ignored, as it is the reverse of what happened to the team in
1992 against the Atlanta Braves, when a hobbling Sid Bream beat
Barry Bonds' throw to home plate to send the Braves to the World
Series instead of the Bucs. In a reversal of roles, this time the Pirates'
star, McCutchen, made a perfect throw to help peg the runner, and
in some ways, reversed the curse of Sid Bream that had symbolically
hung over the city like a dark cloud for twenty-one years. The ball
ricocheted off Byrd in right, was picked up by Cutch who flung it
toward home, was picked up by Morneau, who made a Jeter-esque
flip to Martin, who withstood a collision at the plate to end the game.
I was backing up at home plate ready to throw up, because I thought
I had just blown the game. It was almost as if history was already
written, and we were just actors on the stage. Would I have liked to
punch-out a guy to end the game that night? Of course, but that's
not how it was scripted. The ending was choreographed in a way
that would erase the vile taste that had lingered in the mouths of
Pirates fans since 1992.

Our division, which was deemed the worst in baseball prior to
the start of the season, ended up with the Reds, the Cardinals, and

us, all with ninety or more wins, and it was unequivocally the toughest division in the game. Despite the fact that we were in the playoffs, we wanted to win the division, as it was more advantageous to have a bye than to have a one-game playoff, where everything you worked for could be ripped away from you. To win ninety-four games is no small feat, and despite the fact we ended up second to the Cards and had to play the Reds in that one-and-done, we at least made it to the dance. To see that the Cardinals made it to Game Six of the World Series against the Red Sox, knowing we hung with those guys all season and into the playoffs, is proof of how very close this team is. It could have very easily been us. We had nothing to be ashamed of.

The one-game playoff against the Reds was beyond description. The players called for a "blackout," and fans were encouraged to dress in black. Rally towels were handed out to the crowd as they filed through the gates of PNC Park. It was the most intimidating atmosphere the Reds could possibly imagine playing in, and we knew from the first pitch that this was ours. From the introductions to the final pitch, the place was overflowing with electricity.

The only person in the city who didn't want to go to the game was my son Jayse, who was so into kindergarten that he couldn't have been bothered, which was very "un-Jayse." He ended up coming, of course, as I wanted him to witness this chapter in the family history book. McCutchen's mom sang the National Anthem wearing her "Just Cutch It" t-shirt, and the crowd went ballistic, taking over the lyrics about halfway through the song. The stadium rocked as the words of "The Star-Spangled Banner" were belted out by a crowd of 40,487 rabid Pirates fans.

Cutch and his mom hugged as she finished, and we were off and running. I stood there during the song, knowing we had already won. It was like William Wallace's speech in *Braveheart* with our unit up on the hill ready to pounce on the helpless Cincinnati Reds. They weren't just playing the Pirates; they were playing the whole city. We won the game 6-2, and we were off to the NLDS to play the Cardinals.

There we took a 2-1 series lead, before Wacha and Wainwright shut us down with dominating stuff. There isn't much you can do about that, except to tip your cap and acknowledge that, on that day, they beat us. It's not always the better team that wins; sometimes it's the team that plays better. It's tournament time and the team that gets the hottest and plays the best fundamental baseball wins.

The mood in the locker room following the game was similar to what I felt in 2006 when I came up short with the Tigers. I knew we worked so hard, but it just wasn't meant to be. Everyone was proud of what we had accomplished, and though disappointed, there was no hanging of heads. We knew what we had achieved and knew that we will be back. There is too much talent, heart, passion, and determination to be one hit wonders. It ended too soon and none of us were ready to stop playing. For me, it was a bit of déjà vu, as it was the Cardinals who stood in my way back in '06, and they did it to my team again.

A few days passed and I lived every baseball player's fantasy by playing the role of rock star, even if just for a moment. During the October 11th Pearl Jam show at the Consol Energy Center, Eddie Vedder invited me up on stage to address the crowd and to experience a YouTube moment that was beyond bucket list. With the lights shining on me and the crowd going ballistic, I played air guitar as Eddie and the band played "Whipping." When we finished the song, I was stunned when Eddie presented me with his Fender electric guitar as a gift. Every athlete wants to be a rock star, and every rock star wants to be an athlete. It was an incredible end to an epic season. The concert helped ease the sting of the bitter playoff result.

As another year comes to a close, I look back on the victories and the defeats, both personally and professionally, and I don't have many regrets. Sure, it may not have gone exactly as planned, but there isn't much I would have changed. I won a few more than I lost, or maybe a few less. I tasted victory, yet as of now, I haven't had World Series champagne poured over my head or sprayed in my eyes, yet the taste that will remain in my mouth long after I walk away from the game is still mighty pleasing to the palate.

One of my favorite movies is *Rock Star* with Mark Wahlberg. At the end of the movie, he hands the microphone to the next guy because he's so burned out from being the rock star after finally getting his chance, and he passes that chance on to the next rocker. It will be the same way with me at the end. This game is borrowed. Nothing is promised, and that's really the story of my career, of my life. Everything is what you want to make of it. Huntington said, in reference to me, that a lot of guys would have given up a long time ago. I want this jersey ripped off my back when it's time to leave the game, and that's why I refused to let that day in Goodyear become my exit from the game. I want to borrow this game for as long as it will allow me, and hopefully I'm able to convey that to the other guys in the locker room.

I will leave the game at some point in the not too distant future, and I will know that I played the game the way my dad played it— the way it was meant to be played. It's a game that we borrow, and we have to savor every moment. Though the game was played by thousands before me and will be played by many to follow, I'll know that for the entire nine innings, I played *Just My Game*.